T0198668

INTO THE PURE ...

Tim Nicholls

BALBOA.
PRESS

A DIVISION OF HAY HOUSE

Balboa Press books may be ordered through booksellers or by contacting:

Balboa Press
A Division of Hay House
1663 Liberty Drive
Bloomington, IN 47403
www.balboapress.com
1 (877) 407-4847

Because of the dynamic nature of the Internet, any web addresses or links contained in this book may have changed since publication and may no longer be valid. The views expressed in this work are solely those of the author and do not necessarily reflect the views of the publisher, and the publisher hereby disclaims any responsibility for them.

The author of this book does not dispense medical advice or prescribe the use of any technique as a form of treatment for physical, emotional, or medical problems without the advice of a physician, either directly or indirectly. The intent of the author is only to offer information of a general nature to help you in your quest for emotional and spiritual well-being. In the event you use any of the information in this book for yourself, which is your constitutional right, the author and the publisher assume no responsibility for your actions.

Any people depicted in stock imagery provided by Thinkstock are models, and such images are being used for illustrative purposes only. Certain stock imagery © Thinkstock.

Print information available on the last page.

ISBN: 978-1-5043-0838-0 (sc)
ISBN: 978-1-5043-0839-7 (e)

Balboa Press rev. date: 05/29/2017

To Joy. A garden is never finished.

Special thanks to Jan Hadfield. She was a willing arbiter between ideas and a truly good assistant offering editorial support.

CONTENTS

INTRODUCTION

What is intuition for you?

Knowing your intuitive life, working into the pure energy of your being, is knowing what you know before you know it. Make this the important thing in your life.

It is feeling empowered, meaning your feelings and emotions will be much less challenged. It is asking for guidance from your inner intuitive energy and at times getting stunning results that leave you in no doubt that there is inner power in your hands. There will be rewards.

You don't want to protect yourself by being fearful of what could harm you. You need to rely on your inner self. Try your little-birdie-told-me-so approach, where you "just know" and rely on your hunches. Work with this and see what comes about, and determine whether you can trust your intuition more.

You can get signals from your energy by observing other people who are more in touch with their inner dignity. When you know more about this other person's inner being than you could know in your cognitive mind, then you know you are in an intuitive sense more in touch with your intuition. Knowing before you know.

People observe their dream states and take notice of what the dream is about. When you are asleep, your conscious mind is at rest, so it is time for your subconscious to play! There are signals here. You can be alert to them and listen in. Be aware of them. This is your subconscious, which is giving you your intuition. It's a bountiful thing to have.

Being focused on your inner self, feeling your body mindfulness, and developing meditative skill will give you power to hear and interpret intuitive messages from yourself, to listen to your inner voice. You're working on how much of you is inner work compared to what comes from your ego mind, which is your voice to the world.

There is a lot of information on the Internet defining intuition and giving guidance on how you can better develop your awareness of and benefit from working more closely with it.

This book is about the author's passage of life and things that helped me find the way to realizing the power and benefits of being a more intuitive person. I had vivid awareness of things that would happen at my college. When they took place, I just thought all other faculty members knew the same information. Later in life I became aware that I had strong intuitive skills. A "horse whisperer" (someone with a unique ability to communicate with horses) suggested I might be able to help a young boy who was having difficulty learning. He said he knew I could help. I thought about it but didn't see how I could or would. At a later time, I became aware that I could have helped that boy.

When you have better developed your intuition, you will realize fear is not the answer and hopeful thinking will not get you there either. What you will get is sharp and clear messages of instruction, but it could be that they are muted (you could feel like you're relaxing in a heated pool).

This is intuitive flow. It will become your own confidential secret guidance system. When you are working toward better understanding of your own skill, you should consider that change, such as buying new music or redecorating your home, will add to a different feel. If you can have fun along with creating new things in your life, this will enable you to better reach your inner energy. Observe the results of hunches you have had that guided this activity and this will test how your intuition is doing. This will mean having fun.

When I had a feeling that I should do something, I followed my hunches. It is great realizing that you are developing skills in the passage of your life. For example, the horse whisperer man had been noted in the news for finding lost pets and helping with horse ailments and behavior matters. Horse trainers spoke well of his abilities. I asked him to join me one weekend and sought his training to manage ways forward. He thought I was resistant to his work in the past, but I didn't feel that was so. I just felt then that I had other, more pressing life activities.

He said I might take several weeks to learn his dowsing skill and handed me his pendulum. (Like water divining to find water underground with willow sticks, a pendulum—something on a chain or anything like that—can be used in training. You can program it to turn in a left or right circle, according to whether you ask yes or no questions. If the pendulum does not go in circles but moves forward and backward, then you have a "don't know" answer.)

I was up and flying with it in a few minutes, so that was sorted! It's natural energy from wherever it comes. I feel most people could get some sense of this with help if need be. The more you use this, the more the practice will give you accuracy to getting better answers. I don't use this regularly, as we all can develop various ways to access intuitive energy, as we all do in developing our spiritual self. I found it fascinating to know and to feel in control of these inner energies. My passage of life leads me onward to new understandings in relationships, health, and finances.

Steve Jobs of Apple said to his staff, "Have the courage to follow your heart and intuition ... everything else is secondary."

Into the Pure ... is about that. Allow quietness into your life, be more focused to your inner being, listen to what is given to you, and let life flow.

The book is about the author's passage in life towards an

intuitive understanding of spiritual empowerment. Its vignettes are used to explain what meanings in life have been learned from these experiences.

This book focuses on the metaphysical energy of intuition—of reading the tea leaves, if you like—which tells us what we know before we know it. Learn to live with this, and you have quite a revelation of life itself. Do your business with this, fathom the relationships of life, and get answers.

How to Use This Book

- Read a chapter at a time, perhaps at night, and work on it in the new day.
- Dr. Wayne Dyer, author of Your Erroneous Zones, said he translated Vaishya's Yoga by reading a chapter, going running for two hours, meditating for two hours, and then translating one chapter at a time. That is the way you get through the Indian masters explaining the correct ways to live a life.
- It's serious stuff working out your passage and meaning in life. You will surely prevail, so find parts of the book that speak well to you. These can stay with you as guides. My first Dr. Wayne Dyer presentation received a quick response when he said, "When the student is ready, the teacher arrives." The audience quickly chimed in to the second half of his statement. When you are ready, you will receive.
- Trust in what you have so that you can utilize that power within. You will know before you know. That is intuition. Like Leo Tolstoy in his novella The Death of Ivan Illyich, he writes about a high court judge who considers the consequences of living without meaning. There is a realization or openness to seeing your life in a new light. Seek for that to happen.

- Treat the book as your daily friend. The questions you ask will be more important to your life than those asked by others. This will define the important things you should best seek new understandings from. It's in yourself.
- You must develop empowerment. Have inner control of yourself, which means having a greater place in life. Getting to have greater knowledge and acceptance of your intuition will help you achieve higher levels of empowerment.
- Your prize is the arrival point when you realize the sun always shines within and your intuitive energy is your greatest voice. Accepting this will sustain your life journey.
- Ask and have faith, and you will be heard.

Unleash Yourself

I have read this on the wall of the gym I go to. Unleash yourself. Shall we? Our energy is our life expression keeping us healthy and enlightened. Let's venture through life developing our own greatness. You will know when things are coming together, driven from a different space. An inner space.

I was aware that I was suited to a grey jacket, one of those of natural twill and natural in its fiber. I was visiting San Francisco, exiting the train station, and I saw a shop on the other side of the road. I knew I should visit. I walked in the main door, and on the near right wall was the perfect jacket. Nice find!

Life is there in front of us. Now go find it.

Intuition it is.

CHAPTER I

THE INTUITIVE ENERGIES AND OUR EGO VOICE

In forming ideas/thoughts about our intuitive energies and our ego voice to the world, while both are needed, this book is about finding your way to better use the soulful/intuitive side of your life.

Soul/intuition is about in the present.

Living in the now is about

- acceptance
- intuition
- understanding
- togetherness
- no blame
- peace
- tolerance
- friendship

Ego voice is about "me." Amongst other things, it is about

- our own ideas
- anger
- pride

- being opinionated
- being unforgiving
- doing stuff
- conflict
- self-importance
- intolerance
- self-interest

Knowing intuition is knowing beyond logic, so you can gain insights into new ways of living. We don't know by intellect. Its source is something we haven't been able to determine. Such as it is, you will know your intellect but will not be able to explain it.

Intuition is a higher order of intellect. Working on becoming more aware of intuitive energy is more about how you feel in your heart. Spiritual essence of our lives is reached differently by different people. Some are really intuitive from heart energy. Just knowing before you know. Others will develop techniques to better work with their intuitive selves. Talking with someone who has high order seventh sense skill, a mystical ability, and seeking to find out more of what they do will give you a better understanding of psychic realm. Indian author Osho, a.k.a. Rajneesh, says, "Intuition is the mystic rose that leads you to the ultimate ecstasy, to immortality." He is talking about enlightenment.

Intuition is realizing your potential and knowing beyond logic.

To get started with opening to your intuitive life,

1. You must first decide to be open to your intuitive life and to be okay with it. It finds you, so be prepared to receive it.
2. Keep a journal of key things that you feel, of dreams, and write down your hunches.
3. Find a peaceful and quiet place and imagine things. This is the turning of your energies to inner things rather than the clatter of the outside world.

4. Write down the key questions that you're asking yourself. In time, maybe by morning, you will have revealed and be given the answers. Trust in this to work. You have to be open to the idea. Also, practice writing the questions. You need to be explicit. These questions you ask of yourself will be the most important questions you will answer in your life. The answers will come. They will not be tainted by the outer ego world. They will be only answered to you. The energy is always there.

5. Just listen. Cut off that critic inside you that has to explain everything. Try to have no judgment.

6. Listen to your inner intuition.

7. Find a place in the house, or garden, or on a beach that is peaceful, and ground yourself. Calm contentment is the goal.

8. Be mindful of what has been happening. Be open to it and don't judge it.

9. Just look, observe, and take more notice.

10. Feel your body. Breathe deep and well from your tummy, extending outward.

11. Think of other people and be empathetic. You will learn to better understand people's thinking.

12. If you write down your dreams, you will get in touch with your subconscious, or intuitive part of your brain.

13. Get rid of negative thoughts as much as you can. You don't want to be feeling emotionally negative. People around you will find you tough in life. The opposite is true. Life becomes more of a joy and comfort if your glass is half full!

CHAPTER 2

INTUITIVE NATURAL LIFE

We all need to take our own spiritual journey, and we will find it in different ways, but universal to all is the energy of our self, our soul. It is at a metaphysical level, which can be interpreted as coming from the things of nature. It is comfortable to accept a world beyond the physical plane we know, the God particle too, of things we newly know, and now will know through discovery, but for some people, it is a realm they're hesitant in approaching. Anxiety comes from unfamiliarity. Investigative individualistic people can be attracted to this idea. Dismissal can be from fear. Yet, to learn from masters, and opening opportunities to study life force, we can gain hugely by getting in touch with our real selves. It is no greater than to commune with nature, as it is nature itself. It's nothing to feel strange about. Find naturalness in all we do: find a waterfall, find a good beach. We are there …

Philosopher, speaker, and writer Jiddu Krishnamurti was regarded by many as a great teacher, yet as he said late in his life, "What we learned from him is that we learned nothing." He obviously wants us to make the gesture of finding our self-energy by asking the questions about the meaning of our lives. The answers will come from within, not from the icon he had become.

I became aware of Krishnamurti from chatting with a psychology professor during which he stated that Krishnamurti had the answers to our life being, more than anyone else. It was from this leader that I found my earlier pen name, Kris Jiddhu, a reflection of the man, and finer substance that intuition comes from. (Now it's Tim Nicholls, my actual name.) In reading Jiddu Krishnamurti's work, I was intellectually challenged by him and found helpful ideas that guided my understanding of our passage through life.

How to do this? Study the elements: water, wind, fire, and earth; read the energies. Everyone can use their stronger senses. For me this is touch, the hands. Great power is available to people who can use all senses in a metaphysical search. If you hear, you have pitch, you play, you could make music, absorb music. Take your strongest sense and practice. Just like riding a bike, you will become more adept. Skill for there for you to use, you just need to ask for answers.

For an open quest for understanding the psychic dimension of our being, finding our capacity to "read" what is our true sentient passage of life that we might otherwise not experience. Use it to find helpful pathways, the goals and visions that will set you working on a great path! The sentient being we are will guide and direct our pathway. A conscious take on our lives will have us lined up to conquer certain mountains and take certain paths. As we know by looking back on our lives, we have likely taken different paths from what we might have expected. To have a sense of this sentient path is a real help to accepting a bigger metaphysical picture of our lives, of what our duties are, of how we can make the opportunities in front of us work better. Just a natural and nicer being among the challenges of what we all face day to day.

Radiating a simple energy of humanity, body, and mind will provide answers to life's challenges. For me, a southern hemisphere guy with a penchant for New York, will fly in and Chunnel out from a romantic night in Paris, will walk through a Cappadocia tufa landscape in moonlight, swim about a hurricane hit Pacific atoll, seek to help lepers in India, and teach the youngsters, the journeys you will read of are the springboard to the connecting dimensional ties of the metaphysical realm. Let the intuitive journey tell its stories.

Not all will take the challenge, yet this book ties some lines of thinking together, ones that will assist those like-minded to find an intuitive thirst! Self-help it is.

I have gathered a studied kaleidoscope of life, like we all do, give and take on how much color and dimension we add to the journey. My creative development, called Hotel off the Square, was about living beyond the usual dimensions of a daily life. It was a reflective of the New York boutique hotels and might be compared as a new version of the famous Chelsea Hotel.

It was called Hotel off the Square as it was just feet from the central city cathedral, which was in the main city square in Christchurch, New Zealand. The hotel had a range of room shapes and sizes due to the structure of the building, as some historical trams ran through it at ground level. There was quirkiness and a touch of uniqueness that truly made it different, and as I know, a success. It met people's needs, their wish for comfort, and some positive energy in their lives.

Into the Pure ... is key to the author's adventures, vitality and experiences. Being open to this means being open to spiritual dimension, the real you! Whatever you think of sixth sense, psychic, subconscious, spiritual life, the first step to acknowledge it and be open to it. From there the spirit, the energy of life—the self—will become paramount to your understanding of your being and how it can answer all things.

CHAPTER 3

GENUINE AND UNDENIABLE SPIRIT

Unleash yourself. That was the graphic spray painted on the gym wall. I didn't really take note of that over many years. What do we leave out of our lives? What could we add?

Steve Jobs described his Apple Computer products as ones that bring social change to our global community, driven by highly specialized science and technology experts. Yet he then says intuition made the difference in bringing them about. Jobs was known for traveling to India seeking spiritual experiences.

Quiet focus of the mind is a first step toward meditative space. I sat on my surfboard, felt the beat of the ocean, and waited for a rideable wave. Instinct and intuition will drive a snap decision. Ride the wave. Sometimes there is no time or need for reasoned analytical consideration. Be impulsive. We need to look at life experiences that lead us to greater understanding of the role of intuition in life.

Malcolm Gladwell, staff writer for *The New Yorker*, in his book *Blink*, says, "Snap decisions, instinct, and intuition often lead to better results than carefully considered reasoned analysis."

As Tim Baker in his book *High Surf* notes, businesspeople are interested in the big wave surfer's instincts and willingness to "jump through windows of opportunity as they arise, making sound decisions under pressure and going with the first impulse."

The sense of using the inner energy that gives us information before we know it is the pathway to a spiritual life that uses science to study manifestations of spirit and uses laws of nature to philosophically study the seen and unseen aspects of our lives. It works as a religion, looking at the physical, mental, and intuitive nature of our being, establishing the laws of God without any fixed idea of God.

Being open to spiritual considerations enables us, along with experiences we have, especially with people around us, to establish the intuitive energies of our life.

This is pretty much a white light point of time, such as the surfer being focused neither on the events of the past nor of the future. This is life at the heart of existence, not being resisted against; it is nature. This is the particularly powerful force of our lives.

I came to know that if life is lived with quiet, onward questioning, an openness to new ideas, to creative endeavors and entrepreneurial enthusiasm, life finds you. In my life there was a pattern of this, and I'm not surprised how life has unfolded for me.

CHAPTER 4

HITCH YOUR WAGON
TO YOUR STAR

You need to live in the world that you love.

I will discuss topics that give examples of empowering and enriching our lives.

I came to believe that relating to people, having goals to make things happen, and wanting to be near others to help them was a great way to live your life.

Power, self-importance, chaos, and intolerance is too much head stuff for me. I'm working on being grateful. Just being. Peace and happiness, please. Why not co-happiness? Understanding together.

The brain and mind are distinct areas. They depend on each other.

How do we get stuck on blame, self-importance, and intolerance? That's not loving a life.

Intuition is part of you, and if you want to find the way forward, this is it. Get a glimmer of something great and you latch on to the amazing power of higher intelligence! It's the journey of communicating with your inner self. Like soulfulness and Zen, when paddling on the ocean waves. Intuition brings the peace in the midst of chaos.

The ultimate philosophy is using intuition to help you know why you live and to find your place in the world.

It is about nature. Sometimes in the new light of night, we find the way to be in the moment and discover a new world of existence. Einstein said it was a preview of life's coming attractions. If you have been living in an inhospitable place, then new equality and powerfulness can empower a new life journey.

I listened to and met up with the late Dr. Wayne Dyer, a clinical psychologist who helped people with self-actualization skills, yet time was to lead him to a spiritual representation of what made living alongside a spiritual world, that could provide better human endeavors. His forty-three books since his first, *Your Erroneous Zones,* gave new ideas to how you could structure your life.

His writings were akin to earlier writings of mine, and we wrote in the same genre. On my first connection with him in Maui, I experienced challenging thoughts. We all need to be open to be guided by others.

I had found new space in Hawaii, following suffering a major earthquake disaster in Christchurch City in New Zealand, and a couple of years on, after surgery of my heart to have a new artificial aortic valve put in place.

Now in travels again, I found myself on the dusty drive to the cliff tops of Honolua Bay on the northwest corner of the island of Maui. Winter waves streamed from a wide ocean expanse into shallow water from volcanic rock shelves. You question being in such an environment, yet the power of nature is all supreme, and the occasion to kindle happiness with it is all-encompassing.

From the cliff-top ridges you spot good surfers, powering from the right breaking point, waves ten, twelve, or twenty feet high. Not in summer though. Nature calms. But in winter it is the Holy Grail!

My friends loaned me a slick yellow board—but with advice not to go out at that point. The reef will cut you to pieces, the brown sharks are big and fierce, and pro surfers will ride over you. I did go out. I had seen the website where these local sharks had been tagged and their presence noted when they surfaced from time to time. We shared the area, but as to where they were between each recorded ping was not registered. The power of the ocean's giant waves was all-enforcing. There wasn't room for concern.

I managed to survive for a couple of days out there. Young and old surfers acknowledged we were on the wave together, body boarders with flippers had a place further along the wave, and were getting good play.

On a much bigger wave day I was to be reminded that what the ocean energy gives, the laws of the ocean will take back! It had taken something of a paddle to get outside the wave break, which are big, expansive waters. I was now among the masters. Looking left, I saw a perfect wave, a surfer standing fully in tubular space, in the barrel, as it's known, yet close to rocky coast that was impending danger while giving the wave its precious uplift. I was there, on the wave, off the wave—and then with a broken board, crashing into the reef, washing onto rocky hinterland, and certainly fearing the worst. The following waves were giants, breaking on the rocky platforms just near the surface of the embroiled water. My biggest wipeout on a surfboard!

A damaged body to match the broken board. The doctor said the sea urchin spikes would find their way out, yet it took some weeks and feeling sweaty with a high temperature in a chilly New York until I realized my body was suffering. That last big reef urchin spike extended out enough to withdraw it, and oh, how the body cried relief!

I rode with nature, my mojo back, a happy smile on my face, my existence joyful.

It isn't any different from listening to your inner being, and when you can devise life to focus on self, getting away from the impending torrent of ego life, then you can have a sweet nature. It's about the being of our lives, being found through these activities and self-focus.

I still have the surfboard fin in my study. Life goes on.

CHAPTER 5

WANT TO STAY AHEAD OF THE CURVE?

Let us work on keeping out of traps that are self-defeating. Let us find some new skills to achieve greatness in your world.

You want to be able to see yourself without a label. I call it riding the Zen wave on a new milk road. You are the expert of your own intuition. You know intuitive stuff, like aha moments, eureka times, and saying a little bird told me so when you just knew. It is like knowing before you know.

Intuition, as the communication from your inner self, will point the way in your life with amazing power. You need to get to know it, as a close friend, another voice in your life. It will come out of the blue when you most need it.

An experienced helicopter pilot reported on the intuitive realm that saved the lives of his passengers. They were returning from a film shoot and the tail rotor failed. This is serious for helicopters, and the pilot knew the expected outcome wasn't good. Pilots in such highly- charged situations don't have calm decision-making time, and air-disaster reports find misinterpretation of the aircraft's dire situation by pilots in great stress. A pilot knows that to have altitude will enable him more time to sort out problems.

The situation was dire. The craft had swung around and was moving forward in a sideways position, with some control by the pilot. He had one hand on the main control. His other arm was jammed in equipment behind him that fell during the chaos following the initial rotor failure.

Aware of his demise, he was trying to interpret the zillions of bits of information flowing into his head. He eventually received the internal message of "no hands, no hands! and finally realized these were alerts from his intuitive subconscious. He only had one hand controlling the speed of the main rotor, and while he felt he might be able to bring his craft into a nearby airport, he was also aware that when he made contact with the ground, he was sure to roll sideways with the rotors turning. Death for all was assured.

His other arm was trapped and unusable. He realized that to save his craft, if he got it to ground, he had to cut power to the rotors. These levers were above him, but his other hand was not free to do this. A rapid lesson in helicopter flying was given to a member of the film crew who were on board, and who, on the call from the pilot, pulled the two engine levers above, which cut the engine's power, and the pilot was able to ease the craft down on the airfield, from five meters up. They survived!

It was evident that the pilot had responded to intuition through subconscious messages, in a time of dire need. We wish all pilots in the same stressful positions the same good energies to deal with dire circumstance.

You have to be open to receiving such messages. There are ways to do this: You need to trust in your instincts and intuitive sense, and you must be open to expecting this can happen. It will guide you, but you will have to be open to change, new pathways, and new options of how you live, and that there will be changes.

Of course, being creative will help, so look for ways to be open to new things in your life. This is about understanding the worth of change. I see the portal to greater intuitive sense use as a change process. It moves us forward. The answers to your big questions are within you, so explore, ask, and see what comes in return.

The following could be starting points to taking control of your place in the world:

- how you dress;
- how you organize yourself; and
- how you arrange your bedroom/study/private area.

Be still, and think of the major questions you need to answer. Write these questions down.

Your questions will be the best ones you will ever answer.

The Doors, the famous rock group led by singer Jim Morrison, were named for the "door" that takes us from what we know to what we don't know. Morrison apparently liked William Blake's quote, "If the doors of perception were cleansed, everything would appear as it is, infinite."

We have an ego voice, which we are most aware of when organizing our day. The other voice is our subconscious intuitive voice, the one that saved the helicopter pilot and his crew (mentioned earlier in this chapter)!

When you are in dire circumstances, be aware that you have great support from your subconscious. Trust your instincts and intuition.

CHAPTER 6

TULLY, A RESCUE DOG

We can react to emergency situations just by having the confidence to give it a go. This can be dependent on having experienced enough to get you through the emergency. Some people freeze when faced with such a challenge. Some people say they just reacted because it was the right thing to do (examples of fight or flight).

When the chips are down, it will most likely be the subconscious intuitive energy that puts you into action.

As we are surprised and shocked when something happens unexpectedly, and even more so when it threatens life? Things can happen so fast, and combinations of things can be shocking.

I was walking on the beach at 7:30 on a summer's evening with Matt Jones, a young Fulbright Scholar who had been in the country just five days. We had joined my editorial assistant, Jan, and her larger-than-life Gordon setter dog, Tully, for a "dog's time on the beach." It was a peaceful, warm summer evening, and the sea was calm. The waves were pretty regular.

We had walked a distance and were returning when a woman ran to us, shrieking that a swimmer was out of control and could drown. Matt and I were surfer guys, and it wasn't about decision making but reaction, taking off shirts and running into the surf wearing shorts.

Matt got to Joshua, the out-of-control twenty-year-old. I was concerned that his frantic waving indicated someone else was in difficulty further out. I was worried that a tough rescue swim was in the air. I couldn't spot anyone, and when we got to make sense of things, determining that it was only one person, we managed to bring him back to shore and calm him down.

It was a situation where the swimmer, wearing jeans, was in shallow water, but suddenly he found himself in a rip current of rushing water moving out to sea. This was tied in with a trough of water between sandbars running along the beach. Together these two things made for him being in strife, and he could have drowned. He felt shocked and out of control.

Such is what can happen on a sunny summer's evening. Where was Tully, whose father comes from a background of search and rescue dogs? Well, he was happily exploring the sand dunes. He must have had faith in us to take care of the situation.

Actually, the story is about Tully and more so his keeper, Jan, who suggested the beach walk take place for us and her doggy to enjoy such a great natural environment. Without Tully and Jan, we would not have been about, and the rescue may not have happened. Life is like that. Jan was surprised, as she didn't usually make the beach trip, and it was unusual for her to be there at that time.

We should look at what we're planning in life's activities, to accept that life will call on us to participate more fully. We should be prepared. The woman who ran up the beach with the warning was also very much part of saving the young man's life. Our own previous experience and willingness in that environment was helpful.

When emergency situations arise and there are no prepared, trained personnel available, another order comes into play. Someone has to do something, even if it is just to warn the appropriate emergency services. This is a time that hidden energies come into play. When a crowd gathers but few are reacting to a need, it is the few who can show the way. We know of these scenarios. Hidden energies come from intuition.

The conscious mind can be overcome with urgent matters and

a whole range of tasks. If there is some subconscious preparation, then the likelihood of getting through such emergency situations with success will be increased. A preloaded subconscious intuition prior to these situations will make for greater awareness when you find yourself in such circumstances. Firefighter chiefs know that attending an emergency is about a lot more than just attending the tasks of getting water to the fire!

Ego-based thinking can be problematic. Of course, it will always play an important part. If you are confident, this will get you on the way toward overcoming an emergency situation.

Matt and I had experience in surfing environments. Attending gyms, organizing students in such environments, and a variety of factors gave us greater confidence in that circumstance—and we had Tully dog!

If you're going to be flawed in your thinking, second guessing, and looking for luck, you will not be working with intuitive energy, one that will provide another level of understanding in such dire circumstances.

Your intuition will always be there with the same energy level and the same responsiveness. It is a valuable life force. When we are open to it and better understand that the most important thoughts and beliefs we have will enter our subconscious, then we can work better with and control our thinking.

For one summer day Tully was the reason for a state of affairs that made for people to be about to enact saving life. Matt, the scholar, was well placed to make the rescue. He had just traveled from a US northern hemisphere winter to a New Zealand southern hemisphere summer.

Another circumstance I was aware of involved a fire alarm in a huge condominium in Washington, DC. We were slow to move to the sound of a fire alarm but soon did when we discovered smoke. So many people and their animals were getting down the stairwell.

We met the firefighters as we went through the lobby and they were heading up in the lift! They proceeded to force outward with their hoses, much of the inner part of the apartment on fire. My friend was a staff member at the White House and showed quick attention to where the head fire person in charge would be. Of course, he was a distance from the building observing, making summation, reacting using all his past training and experience. No second-guessing for that man.

Such is the power of getting organized in your own being, the skills you know are important and are necessary in emergency circumstances. Intuition is a very useful attribute to have in such a situation.

CHAPTER 7

WHEN THINGS GO WRONG

Life could be like waiting for the crocodile to surface in a murky swamp, but that won't help much to advance a good and successful life. Things can go wrong in very short spaces of time.

We were on a school hike and traversing a rocky outcrop with a steep entry uphill. The fourteen-year-old students were on a full-day challenge as part of an outdoor education camp. As teaching master in charge, I was at the tail of sixty-six students, most of whom had moved past the outcropping.

A call rang out! A student had overbalanced a large rock, which came thumping toward us. David, the boy on my right, looked up and was hit in the forehead, indenting one side into the other, and immediately fell into a coma. Everyone was shocked.

I held him in my arms, working to not slip down the slope. The other two staff were instructed to leave six capable students to help, get the rest of the students off the mountain, and raise the alarm.

We spent the first twenty minutes taking stock of a very serious situation. A rope was tied around me so I could be supported with David. We all lifted our classmate up to a ridge, where we could take stock of the situation.

How would you react in such a situation? What would you rely on to manage?

There was a warm but strong wind. We busied ourselves putting our patient into a recovery position and building a vegetation cover of bushes to protect him from wind chill. I positioned myself over him in a protective arch to try to maintain temperature and monitor his reactions. He moaned from pain and was vomiting. I knew it was serious, but he was alive and we could look after him as best as possible. Help would come.

Three hours passed, and while we could view a long way in the distance, there was no sign of help being organized, and not knowing was disconcerting.

I sent the fittest athlete of the six assisting students to seek further help, and this fellow, Shane, set off to find a road and get a message through that we needed a helicopter. I felt rescue after dark would have increased risks of David not surviving.

Shane ran and ran, and a military truck of soldiers on maneuvers found him running down a road. Shane was covered in sweat. The soldiers, on returning to base, sent a message to police, and an air force rescue helicopter was sent.

It was five to six hours since the accident, and students reported hearing a thudding sound. I raised my head into the wind and the sound disappeared. Head down again and there was a consistent thud, with which this Iroquois helicopter came over the ridge nearby. Not immediately spotting us, it started its search, and when they spotted a red jacket being waved, they came directly to our location. I indicated a flat area for them to land, and they put the skids down but kept the engine holding in a hovering pattern.

After some time, a medic crew came around to where David was, and intensive medical care and rescue began. I was very happy to leave the mountain on foot with the five other students. The rescue was successful.

David survived, and after a stay in hospital, was able to convalescence at home; he made a good recovery. On that day the police sent out a rescue party of local farmers using the police's Land Rover, carried a stretcher, and reached a position just below the rocky outcrop where the incident happened.

The rescue by land was happening despite my fear that it may not. The air rescue was right for the seriousness of the situation. How good a team everyone had been, and especially the students who stayed back to assist.

What is learned when all mental faculties are challenged when such an event occurs? There will be immediate logistical matters to be decided on, yet amazing power will come from your intuitive self, and you need to acknowledge it. Amazing power is available. Glimmers and hunches will come from your higher intelligence. A feeling, such as gut reaction, images, or hearing of messages, such as in dreams, will all be part of this side of your life. Become familiar with all your power of your inner self by listening to it.

Look within. Accept that help can and will arrive from this source. Take notice of strong feelings when it doesn't necessarily make sense. You don't need to question intuition, but you do ask questions of it.

CHAPTER 8

BE QUANTUM INTUITIVE

When our sensory behavior jumps from one point to another with no clear in between, we have an aha moment. It is much more complicated than that. It's a bit more edgy. You need to have faith in new understandings of how life works.

In biology, subatomic particles can do two or more things concurrently or be entangled with distant partners. It's not all togetherness out there! Sometimes things dematerialize here and instantly turn up elsewhere. Do tunneling and coherence take place? This is complicated stuff that scientists are investigating. Cells in the body can maintain quantum states, which are finely balanced and keep some edge between the world we know and the quantum world we are discovering.

I will tell you of a tale of where things went wrong. We were a group of students with a leader passing through Sea-Tac Airport in Seattle, en route to a conference in San Francisco. The topic was conflict resolution, based on the United Nations year of conflict resolution.

Passing through security, the alarm went off as Sam, a young, intelligent sixteen-year-old boy in our group set off a chain of events. He had bought a simple toy-shaped gun device with wooden clothes pegs for the action sounds. The poor woman on the screen detection had no option but to freeze the moment! Police and security people came running, and Sam was drilled for some time, trying to explain what was going on. Airport operations stopped. The train system froze. We all watched with concern.

In San Francisco the conference carried on, and our time to present was starting to look shaky. The airport eventually hummed into life, and two students and I ran for the plane, made it, transported to the San Francisco venue, and gave the talk. Our fellow member was still with authorities in Seattle and was being watched over by close associates of ours. We had closed the airport down. But things carry on in another stream of life, and the day was to take place within planning but without the expected process we had anticipated.

This was about my way of understanding how things related can be going on in different places at the same time. It's a bit haphazard in thinking but fits the idea that all things connect, and onward to universal connection.

Our cells have that propensity to change their spread and cover more channels of movement than the one you would expect. Once the cells have spread to traverse via these various channels, they determine their best route. Linking in mysterious ways, Einstein referred to them as "spooky."

Life finds ways to move, transform, and reorganize itself. The above example of closing down an airport through some innocent folly didn't stop the flow to complete the day as planned. Sam rather sheepishly turned up at the event some hours later and what was, was best left for reflection. In our world there are similar patterns that help to better understand the quantum. Life does find ways to move, transform, and reorganize itself. I feel intuition is very much part of this process.

In intuitive life, what may appear as black and white often is not. Universal energy is just that, for all of us. We are all the same. We are one.

CHAPTER 9

THE BLACK CAT AND OTHERS

Does your cat or dog speak to you in milliseconds? When I'm about to go for a ride in the car, Snuky and Poppy, the neighbor's dogs who visit often, react in a millisecond when I indicate a journey is being organized.

Humans have millisecond jumps of alertness to information. There is no information cognitive overload, just pure wisdom from your subconscious. This guidance is within, and we need to listen. The questions we ask ourselves are the best ones we will ever have, and our intuitive sense is one of the best guides we have available.

The black cat was among seven Burmese and Siamese cats belonging to a neighbor. Black Cat, as she came to be known, made herself part of our place next door, and she did so quite insistently. In time, we had to inform the neighbor that his cat was living at our place. A good man, yet his response was akin to her being a silly cat. Cats know where to go and live.

Black Cat had a good life and attached herself to a senior member of the family. When this matriarch died, the cat waited daily for her to turn up. A horse whisperer told me that Black Cat could sense her keeper and became confused when she didn't appear.

Black Cat could tell us a lot if we were able to converse. She had that special quality of just knowing before she knew. This is what intuition is. It doesn't need rational explanation. We need faith to work with this powerful force of our being.

Following a major earthquake disaster, many cats disappeared, many to nearby hills. There were many more reports of missing cats before the first earthquake hit. Missing animals doubled in preceding weeks, and the rate was five times higher the day before the first big earthquake. Results were statistically significant. Many returned upwards of a year or more on. Some obviously found new homes. People set up websites to share information of animals found.

There were stories of cattle lying down in the paddocks before the earthquake period started. It is believed there is possible change in behavior due to electromagnetic fields created by increasing pressure on rock.

Six donkeys were heard braying early in the morning before the 4:38 first big quake, which caused the earth to move 6.5 feet vertically and horizontally. Some animals react at earthquakes, but how far from normal is difficult to quantify.

Cats pawing at owners minutes before a quake is convincing behavior.

Pheasants seem to respond more than other birds. There is always unfamiliar bird behavior, and spirals of birds flung out of trees in a counterclockwise direction before the earthquake struck.

Babies have great connection to subconscious life, and in their first nine months, they could tell us a lot about their subconscious world. Thereafter they learn the human skills of the ego mind, the voice to the world around us.

There is much around us that can alert us to take better care of our intuition. Things that hold us back are ego ideas. Establishing strategies to move forward with better intuitive understanding will make us better placed for connecting to the world beyond us. That is what the animals do.

CHAPTER 10

ENCOUNTER/MEDIA: WHEN HUMANS CHANGE THE NATURE OF HUMAN INTERACTION

I had an unusual experience when I was a young university student. At a national universities arts festival, we had an experiential social psychologist in attendance.

This was an exercise whereby the greater subconscious energy comes to the fore. This has been of concern that such sensitivity-training encounter group activity is dangerous for those who are susceptible to mental problems, although statistics indicate that the same number applies to equivalent populations.

The encounter session was probably not meant for a general audience. Perhaps the arts festival for university students was an appropriate venue. The task was to find other people to communicate with, despite operating in blindfold. Once two had connected, there was a quest to add another couple and eventually a group of eight. We used all our senses except for sight, and that changed things.

After a long process certain inhibitions were removed, and we all behaved like a bunch of kids. The ego strictures had been wound down. The inner being was the force. It was fun in its difference, and it was scary in its challenges.

I was a student representative, and at a later time I was in a chat with our campus health professionals who were concerned about the number of students who needed counseling following the encounter exercise. What this told me was that we are not all of the same mettle to handle such immediate challenges. Those of us who have gone through earthquake disasters know that some people are much more effected by such challenges.

If we think about it, an earthquake's shock waves go right through you in a way that is different from other experience. There will be a percentage of people who are more challenged by that. Others on the continuum of behavioral responses will vouch for it as nature unlocking its energy in a strident way and accept it is nature as we have to know it. You are the master of your intuitive energy.

For those who want empowerment from within, unleash yourself! Voyage to yourself. There, the sun always shines.

This was part of my journey, which told me more about how our inner selves work.

You are the master of your intuitive energy.

In media, there is power. Politicians who use that well are adept at understanding the ways that it can be effectively used. Take a TV studio with a camera. As TV presenters, we talk about looking down the barrel. You have a focus: it's the camera. How can you use this and be natural as in the kaleidoscope of a normal life? Our trick was to imagine that we were having a conversation with someone at home on the family couch.

You have to be focused to that angle with the camera and "charge ten thousand volts" to be something more than of usual human disposition. There is no proscenium arch, like an arch framing the opening between the stage and the auditorium in some theaters. You have to focus on a place, such as the camera.

When reading news, I didn't feel I could convince someone to buy a used car from me! I was that unconvincing. It made more sense for me to be behind the camera, which led to an interesting life with media communications and journalism that eventually led to Fulbright Scholar research. It was a major part of my intuitive life passage.

CHAPTER 11

CREATIVITY AND INTUITION

What are we doing when we're creative? When we have a new idea and a manageable concept, and then maybe put it into an entrepreneurial process, what are we doing? I'm going to suggest that the start of a process is first about opening to newness. Change is implicit here. What could be different? Now you want a eureka moment. Not considered analytical thinking but very much of the "a little bird told me" type of nuance. The eureka moment will be just great! It just comes to you. From where? From your subconscious intuitive energy. Be open to that.

Great ideas just appear when we have placed ourselves in a position for that to happen. The implied thought could lead to what takes the process many steps further. The entrepreneurial part is the business mode you follow to market the created goods or service. I was often asked how I design hotels. Am I an architect? No, and I paid off some architects who worked for me. That is a different process.

"I design from the earth," I say, which is like architect Frank Gehry's process. His pen stayed on the page until intuitive understanding came to the fore.

It needs you to open to your self-energy, the intuitive energy and stride to pure form of information. Look inside and use what you find to open outward, record what information comes along, and use it to manage the outside world.

I asked my film/television students to think as widely as possible for ideas of a film we could make. We would be at the unmanageable part that was unattainable in actual filming, just stretching the imagination too much, but necessary.

Only by venturing to the beyond of ideas that might have seemed crazy did we find ourselves in a more manageable creative zone. Stretch the imagination first, I say.

Looking at cities could be a way to determine change factors that make for greatness. Barcelona took a stride forward in making itself a great Olympic city. Not only is the old mixed with the new, but cruise lines and modern facilities can be seen alongside the Basílica Sagrada Família (Antoni Gaudi's cathedral) and other superlative buildings. Why and how? The thinkers in that city at that time managed a creative change model that drove the project to greatness.

It comes from within. Their attitude was the key thing. This is the most important aspect of greater use of intuitive life. You have to be open to it!

Another pleasure of my long visit to Barcelona was the professional quality of the dining service, waiters, and waitresses—just superb! I mentioned it to a lady alongside me who worked at the US embassy. My message was that they are first-class service providers. In Spanish, she let them know I was a hotel owner and creative developer.

When told I was impressed, their retort was, "That's what we do."

The next day they sent a message that they would like to come and work for me in New Zealand! We did have a tapas bar in the newest hotel, but alas, we didn't manage to make this happen.

Following the dinner, the wait staff all lined up outside the entrance to see us off. In my Kiwi manner, I was happy to move along, chatting with them and acknowledging the pleasure of truly professional service.

This was again part of my passage, and I was taken with the sense that this was an inner understanding that provided for the level of service. Probably from a long history of building on those skills.

I was in the Catalonia region with a group of US CEOs on a study mission organized by the Seattle Trade Alliance. We were often in university and city building that had been adorned by work of Antonio Gaudi. To be able to glance upward at truly superlative artwork, during a lunch presentation, was truly amazing.

Some thinking is that creativity has to be encouraged by being alongside other likeminded people so that your network power is greater.

I can think of people working isolated from that type of a place and still becoming a Nobel prize winner, which I will discuss further.

CHAPTER 12

SERENDIPITY

Serendipity is about putting yourself in a position so a sudden connection will surprise you.

For example, go travel in Nepal, and be open to everything around you. You will be met with surprise. You'll know something is happening that was meant to happen. You have a big part to play in serendipitous happenings.

I arrived at Kathmandu Airport, and there in the outer crowd was a sign with my name on it. Surprised, I thought I should ask because I hadn't signaled that I was going to be in Nepal. Yes, the sign was for me, and I was whisked off to the Kathmandu guest house.

Days later in another part of Nepal, I was asked by another traveler, "What makes you a VIP?"

I downplayed it but discovered that the staff had been told at the Kathmandu guest house that I was to be looked after or there would be trouble! Ouch! Not what I would encourage. Serendipity? No. Just a New Zealand friend from a government organization letting someone in Nepal know that I would be arriving.

Do you have to fail in creative endeavors to find the best answers? I don't think so. Failure is a learning aspect for sure. Being open to new ideas will assist greatly. Being able to acknowledge choices open to you when they arise will make for creative opportunity. Be open-minded in your operation of life and you will have success.

Analogous would be the car driver who mostly only sees what is ahead and maybe some of the things to the side, compared to the driver who is constantly aware of activity all around the car.

Walking on a busy street or through an active shopping mall will be an advantage if you have this sense. Business operators have great success when they are, all things considered, high on reflection and knowing in their beings of a greater realm in which to work.

CHAPTER 13

SURFING

In *Just Add Water: A Surfing Savant's Journey with Asperger's,* about Clay Marzo, the young global surfer with Asperger's syndrome who lives in Maui, Hawaii, author Robert Yehling gave recognition to "what purity of joy and expression look like in the flesh."

Yehling sees muscle memory as a great sacred gift for Marzo and gives reference to "the 360-degree view Clay uses to see and feel how everything feeds into the moment and to anticipate it." The Asperger's diagnosis of this surfer has provided for interest. He clearly operates at a higher platform. I believe that intuition and muscle memory, knowing before you know, validates his mastery on a surfboard and provides the mystique of huge talent that is Clay Marzo.

My life has been influenced by surfing. Marzo's story emanates from a place in Hawaii I have lived in and connected with. It speaks of what I have come to know. There is a powerful inner awareness when people participate in big-scale ocean environments than just being there. The beat and energy of the ocean is immense in many dimensional ways. To me this "speaks" in my passage of life as a life force that is key to the intuitive self. It is life, the source of being. Big statements, but meaningful in understanding our inner being, what life is all about.

In Pacific Ocean folklore, Maui was a god in the realms of

cosmology and creation, say Hilary and John Mitchell of Mitchell Research. John was a senior lecturer in psychology at the University of Canterbury in my undergrad time. Their master research work was *Te Tau Ihu o Te Waka: Te Tangata me Te Whenua (the Prow of the Canoe: the People and the Land), volume 1 of 4*. This work details the rich history of Maori of the Nelson and Marlborough regions of New Zealand, with reference to the wider areas of Samoa, Tahiti, and Hawaii. They weave together political and oral histories through fabulous tales about Maui. (Interestingly, John's full Maori name is Maui John Mitchell, his father having Te Morehu Maui as part of his name. They were named after Sir Maui Pomare of Taranaki, a famous New Zealander.)

Chatting over lunch with Mike Resnick, who has a long-time connection to Kahana, Maui, the similarities in cultural tales and language is warming and satisfying to understanding our place in the world, and it is generated far and wide. A young couple, New York friends of Asian descent whose child was conceived from this place in Maui, add to the crossing of paths in the world. It's a precious mix of global heritage. And it shall be, that we are all as one. These things speak to me, as meant to be, understandings from my passage of life. Culture, heredity, connections such as the Polynesian reference makes for very connected elements of our being and in that a big intuitive life sense, so be open to it.

Being aware of people around you is a life opportunity that may just lead to great creative opportunities.

I wrote about a guy carrying a stack of boxes at Union Station, New York, who lost his grip. I didn't help. I think I was too shy. Yet I have never forgotten the occasion, nor the image of the person, and I know we were meant to connect. His look and the energy of that moment said as much.

Be open to it. It can pass you by and you will never know. It's meant to be. Meant to be that shyness and being in a new cultural environment meant what should have meant to be did not. The point I am making is that you need to look around, acknowledge such moments of connection, and connect! Be aware of who is actually around you.

I was walking through the West Village in New York City on the way to meet a friend who was a head waiter. I was walking quite fast, yet suddenly I caught the eye of a woman dining with her companion on a sidewalk café. She leapt to her feet, and we embraced in a wild acknowledgement of meeting. We had never known each other, yet we both knew instantly that we were meant to meet. That was exciting! It emerged that she had been on a photo shoot at the Soho House and Club, of which I was familiar, and the supervisor of the film shoot was a guy I had known some years before. Explain it? No. Just accept that such inner awareness is meant to be and represents greater things. To me it is intuitive life.

CHAPTER 14

NOBEL PRIZE

Alan MacDiarmid grew up in Masterton, New Zealand, a long way away from many centers of innovation and industrial revolution change. From a relatively poor background, he took a part-time position as a "lab boy," or janitor, at the University of Victoria in the capital city of Wellington, as he studied for a BSc, MSc, and then a Fulbright Scholarship at the University of Wisconsin-Madison. He was studying inorganic chemistry. He went to Cambridge in 1952, where he finished a second PhD in 1955. He researched at Scotland's University of St. Andrews, Scotland, the University of Pennsylvania, and in 2002, at the University of Texas at Dallas. With all this elite academic work, he was expert in conductive polymers and was able to conduct electricity in plastic materials that led to such things as the cell phone screens we now have.

When he was in Wellington in those early days, he witnessed an experiment that had gone wrong. He remembered a yellow material that had come from a reaction in the lab. Many years later, when visiting a Japanese research center, he spotted the same yellow reaction in a student's work.

"What did you do?" he asked.

After overcoming the language difficulty, the student replied, "I only did what I was told." His response was worked through, and it became apparent that the quantities had been changed by some ten times. This eureka element led to a Nobel prize in chemistry in 2000, and Alan MacDiarmid, in his last period of lectures, made us aware of the power of globalizing the effort of innovation. So, networking can add to further change, but isolated instances anywhere, any place in the world can be the start of a Nobel prize win!

Eureka moments are moments of time of the intuitive energy. It is a quick jump from one element to another, no deduction, just knowing. You will know eureka moments in your life. Acknowledge them as intuition. Ask questions to access them.

CHAPTER 15

THE UNIVERSAL CONNECTION OF PEOPLE

The connection of people is greatly universal. You can find common life concerns wherever you go. What people want is enough resources to survive, protect their children, have access to education, etc. The major differences pale to being not so great, except when they are manifest into conflict and death, such as the present history of radicalism that has found a place in the contemporary world. It's politics within and around belief systems.

The answer will be for moderate believers everywhere to show the way. To see furthest will be the highest you can go. The reason for new forms of entrepreneurial endeavors that have become major agent changes in the world (for example, Apple, Microsoft, Google, and Facebook) is the source of historical era of younger voices being heard. This was from the 1960s into the '70s when emerging youth found their voice. The events of the time show sit-ins at universities, students taking up political issues, from apartheid South Africa to East Timor, to the Vietnam War. Young voices were being heard, and changes in society and the world were duly affected. There was a radicalism to much of it.

The PLO (Palestinian Liberation Organization) cause led to plane hijackings; the Red Army in Germany struck out; and within the United States were outbursts in the helter-skelter period of

Charles Manson and his followers. There was discourse worldwide, yet there was change that brought new voices and participation. From this came the dot-com foray of business and the new social media platforms.

In another age the youth voice in universities has become centralized and mellow in comparison, and radical forms in the nature the Arab Spring and ISIS have replaced young people's voices of the past with regressive beliefs and terrorist actions.

In Christchurch City, New Zealand, a major earthquake saw 70 percent of the central business district demolished. The east side of the city was very much affected by the liquefaction process of underground sandy silts being forced up to the surface. It needed to be removed. A "student army" of university students made themselves available to help with recovery efforts, and they have been commended for their efforts.

Action among young people—yet you will not find the same strident political call on issues of the time that were the reflection of issues in the past, so looking in advance, it mellows the thinking about what unique developments could surface at present. It raises the question about what is necessary. While global waves of change come from and are enacted out locally, can we expect local initiative to be a precursor to what the world needs globally? The Palestinians still languish, the Pakistanis suffer all sorts of radicalism evolving out of the Middle East, and for the present, the ISIS beliefs cause mayhem throughout the Middle East and Europe.

It is somewhat perplexing as to the true reasons for all this more recent history as the issues are vital and complex. There are many factors. But there is inward radical thinking of young leaders who feel dispossessed of the resources and opportunities that they feel are rightfully theirs. If a vision of a well-off America was part of the arising of the horror attack in New York of 911, then the lack of access to resources leading to political impotence of youth that led to the Arab Spring was certainly of some simplicity in the understanding of what has been going on. Of course, neither is excused for the immense amount of human loss and suffering that the world endures from it.

Within each of these minds of malcontent individuals is an external view of the world that labels race, privilege, power, lack of access to alternatives, and finding place as just some of the reasons for vicious discord. The paradigm of peace can be found by looking onward at the love, pureness, and common sense that prevails when people open the way for intuitive understanding. It's from the person, inward, that outward manifestation of good sense to solve problems can surface.

I was a student politician and all these areas were of immense interest. They follow on as political interests in my life. It is my passage, my being.

The great teacher Jiddu Krishnamurti would be happy to see world leaders fall into a line of intuitive understandings of the energy of our being and acceptance that we can all find in divine spirituality, enough to feed our souls and make for peace. A fuller study of his work will illuminate the realm of being in our lives, the most important question we have to answer, and he is possibly of the most enlightened humans to express that.

As the world leadership seems to regress in many places, the hopes for such resilience and sanctity of life is seemingly lost. Good energies need to surface to make our lives meaningful. We must progress to the pure …

E kore e heke heke he kakano rangatira.

Our ancestors will never die, for they live on in each of us.

CHAPTER 16

CLOSE READ: THE MEDIA

The adventure in finding a passage in life that takes into account that that there is something larger than ourselves is a good step forward, as it removes the likelihood of analysis/paralysis of action.

Having a relaxed body and calm mind is meditation. You can experience this following exercise, such as working out at the gym or walking in the park. Isn't a beach a great place to feel and smell realness? You will not get meditative benefits from sleeping, praying, going over affirmations, nor from the ideas of positive thinking. Not even daydreaming or thinking is meditation. Don't think of it as reading the newspaper or watching sitcoms you like.

You need to acknowledge awareness of simple focus of your attention to simple things. You need to get your breathing right. Turn your mind away from what is going on external to you. That's the ego voice part of all this. Get to the body, mind, and heart. You want to think of pure being beyond the mind. Be Zen and get connected to one part of the body. Be mindful to that, or meditate with all the body, inclusive to relaxing, with further focus on senses: smell, touch, and so on. Just be open to it. Comfortable position, clothes, music. There are lots of aspects to great meditation, but being mindful over five minutes will get your mind focused on the echelons of inner being. Being mindful or meditative will take you inward to your inner energies, and hence, you will be in the intuitive realm of your life.

I was more specialist in media, communications, and journalism. It's all-encompassing of huge realms of life. It's also really weirdly attached to, among other things, fame, self-importance, controlling the information, and self-aggrandizement. How do you cope with life when fame and public awareness take over? Some cope. Many fail dismally.

I was involved in CBS news in New York, and the scale of operation is large for TV stations. High-powered. Sitting in the control room at evening news time was a full-on onslaught. The director was running a marathon and casting new language as a driven crew kept focused and acute to the cause. I would see this type of control room again in the movie *The Insider*, starring Russell Crowe, about the whistleblower of the tobacco industry.

Across the road was the *60 Minutes* program's directors and team leaders. Now here was a job I would like—take a crucial and topical exposé in society and develop a program about it. A crew had just returned from a southern city covering police problems. The police had tried to find the crew and run them out of town. When Hurricane Katrina hit, the supposedly missing police was partly due to having phantom names on lists. They couldn't look after people because they didn't exist. Well, that was the talk on the street.

The media has a responsibility in alerting us to these problems, not to curry favor to any one side. It may not suit all people, but that's it. What is needed to have people media aware is a closer understanding of what is between the lines. What did the newsmaker and gatekeepers set out to do, and how can the individual see more transparently what the true messages really are?

So, we do close readings, which is the media literacy that all students deserve to have at some stage so they can interpret the reality of what is behind the news production. Once the media only play from the middle keys of the piano, it's analogous to leaving out what you really need to know. So you need to be able to ask the real questions.

This was significant passage of life for me to further reach intuitive life. Knowing between the lines of a close media read is akin to knowing in yourself that intuitive life is driving your day to day decisions.

The media has a responsibility role in defining and alerting us to these problems, not to curry favor to any one side. It may not suit all people, but that's it.

For example, there has become a horror in social media where the slitting of throats and cutting off of heads by ISIS militants has been viewed on social media. There are no traditional gatekeepers to decide what makes for good sense. Those were the editors, subeditor, chief reporters. Some adolescent students took the opportunity to view those events via the Internet. What was to be the effect on their ongoing lives? Could the images ever be taken away?

Knowing what we know in an intuitive sense is that, not very injurious to the inner you. Media students—in fact, all students—should have media literacy to a level that equates to the challenges that are arising. Does humankind have the strength to manage these enormous challenges that beget whether life is held? With test tube medicine, a new reality emerges. I believe that the human race, by its experience of reacting to global challenge such as AIDS and bird flu, find ways to best manage, so onward. I will cast a vote for "We can do it!"

CHAPTER 17

MEDICAL PROCEDURES

I just visited Robert, an in-law and friend who had a heart procedure to replace the aortic valve in his heart. He looks okay, yet he has come through a major event in his life. There are protocols for this work. Dr. David Shaw did the same operation on me. I could share the event Robert went through and add some comments to help him along. It will take two weeks to get over the initial shock and for the body to readjust, and then, over the next couple of years, there will be effects from the surgery. There may be fibrillation of the heart, as there are irregularities and speeding up of heart chambers and their operation. There may be depressive effects. He had a specially bred pig valve implanted. I have a synthetic aortic valve. I need to take Warfarin daily to keep the blood thin, so that there is no coagulation on the synthetic valve. There are protocols for this procedure, followed all over the world, and bringing life to people who have had heart valve failure.

When people have heart problems, they may have stents, a small tube inserted up blood canals to the relative part of the heart system that needs to be kept open. Quick help.

For some, a bypass, maybe as much as a quadruple bypass, is necessary, where surgery of the diseased heart needs help by using arteries, which are stitched around a beating heart. This brings life.

The valve surgery may not be of a diseased heart but where a valve has failed and blood is not controlled well from the heart.

The procedure surgically cuts open the body to temporarily stop the lungs and heart, divert blood flow, and stitch in a new valve. I am describing a lay person's simplified explanation of what happens. People ask me about this, and this is it, the way surgeons and heart specialists give you increased life. The anesthetist's explanation of risk was that it was of a level equal to the dangers of being a pedestrian around car traffic over six months. This is manageable and in life akin to managing risk. You know you are in good hands.

People often ask me of the symptoms that alert you to the fact that you need help, other than a sudden heart attack. They affect people in different ways. Besides the usually considered chest pains, others had continuous coughing, a sense of stomach discomfort, and so on. You can't be sure of anything! But if you feel in your intuitive sense that something's not right and that you need help, then you need to seek help. Ask your GP. Go to an emergency ward and discuss the use of an echo test (echocardiogram) to know how the heart valves are functioning. Shortness of breath is also a major sign.

The body is wonderful in compensating to overcome major illness, so a sudden collapse can happen when this has reached its limit. Your best aid is to trust your intuition. If you feel you have a problem, you will not be wrong to have it checked. This can be your savior. I say this because this is the most likely way that you will determine you have a problem and are more likely to seek medical help by acknowledging it. From my heart experience, I see this as the most important force in seeking medical help. Many heart problems lead to death because the above is not followed. In discussing with surviving patients, intuitive alertness to the problem made for successful medical assistance and life itself! Intuition and successful medical treatment go hand in hand to successful treatment. Understanding the work of the heart specialist and heart surgeon, which includes a complex field of science that guides their work, exceeds the scope of this book.

You can be a good student of the relative factors that make your situation better understood, but there is inner realm stuff that we can't easily read. On being released from intensive care following major open-heart surgery, which will take a morning or afternoon, I was walked from the intensive care area to my room, so that my body could sense and start the journey again of living! Pure wonderful living. Time to soar! Well, it will be so after an adjustment period and maybe a couple of years will see continuous improvement, but with an up and down journey.

Usual life does that too. Feel good today, not so much tomorrow. It is all a journey.

The surgeon said to me, "I will do the work in the operating theater and carry out the procedure. I will take care of you. When I see you later in your room, I want to see you doing the work of healing. Sit up, get going, be active."

This tells you there is a great deal more to this process of gaining life than the part of renewed "plumbing" in the heart.

CHAPTER 18

GETTING YOUR MOJO BACK

Mojo, what I regard as inner being, that which gives us inner identity, soulful feel, drive, and a way forward in our spiritual being takes a big knock when an incursion into our body structure and processes, such as major surgery, takes place. I feel that in some way the patient needs to get this back. It may be noticed as a lack of confidence. It is about motivation. It could be what psychologists call self-actualization processes. This is onward life that you as the patient is very much in control of. I was affected by atrial fibrillation and had to be taken to hospital by ambulance, but in several hours the doctors had stabilized me. I was released later that night after five hours.

I then walked to the intensive care unit, where a young nephew was in a coma from an accident where a car had crossed the center line and smashed head first into his car. He survived but with head injuries that needed months of careful attention. As a court prosecutor, his work life was going to be affected.

An intensive care specialist who had assisted me came by and commented that this event would affect me. I thought otherwise, but now I accept it as so. I suffered depression over a couple of years. This wasn't as serious as looking down a tunnel that seemed impossible to escape. I experienced despair and panic. The solution is to find a way to do so, so that you are confident about managing that another time. None of that for me. Just a malaise that made the first half of the day difficult to get active, yet the second half of the day was active at twice the pace! What was going on?

As a student patient, as I saw myself, the pathways I had been able to traverse in life were important to the future. A challenge to reconnect to these xis good. That will guide the way.

I see my passage of life with reference to the open-heart surgery and the Honolua Bay surfing incident as closely related in determining how we see our inner life processes, and the significance of how we personally handle these occurrences. Open-heart surgery, depression, and surfing big waves with success and demise were all very connected for me in coming to understand inner being.

In another part of the book, I write of surfing Honolua Bay in Maui, Hawaii. I just revisited that by Googling "surfing Honolua Bay early 2016," and there was vivid film from above, of big waves this year, akin to my experience getting my mojo back. For I was pushing the boundaries on a twenty-foot wave run and suffered a broken board, being thrown onto the reef, dragged along the sharp volcanic rocks, and escaping with my body intact but with some reef vegetative spikes in my hand.

I had surfed there over some days and had announced my comeback to friends far and wide. Many passed on comments of "well done." Now I lost my feeling of achievement and worth of inner being. You might say these are loose descriptions. This is the inner realm of our lives that we know exists. That can't be quantified and analyzed. It's just life!

I came to terms with the challenge of this. With a general sense of heightened spirituality, it is possible to see the challenge of coming to terms with such an event in your life as a growth matter and to this end, an achievement of mojo itself. Be open and you will see it as you need it. It comes your way. The surgeon's guidance, that healing was up to me, extended into these other realms. Be intuitive to this. Clearly this is development of your spiritual being and hence I see intuition adding to your greater spiritual being and beliefs and understanding in good energy that you may make important to your life. It is choice. It is belief. There is also science. The science of intuition.

Open-heart surgery is going through changes. Computer-generated views of the inner heart amplified ten times allow surgical instrument work controlled externally by surgeons. The invasive nature of this procedure can be reduced by entering through the ribcage.

CHAPTER 19

OPEN-HEART SURGERY

There is adventure in taking into account that that there is something larger than ourselves.

That is a good step forward, as it removes the worldly ego voice as the only precursor about what will happen to us as life proceeds. If the universe is in us, then we have the best guides within us. We just have to listen.

It happened to me. A new aortic valve was sewn into my heart. I was "sleeping." The surgeon was in control of the procedure.

Was it due to the rheumatic fever from when I was eleven? Probably just wore out, said the surgeon. I had gone through a period of stress with earthquakes and other disasters.

While celebrating New Year in Bangkok, some young New York friends gathered, and we all had a great time in the National Park northeast of Bangkok. We walked to a waterfall, and on climbing back up steep ancient block steps, I was gasping and felt faint on reaching the top. Could it be the food from yesterday? I asked. No, actually, it was a major heart problem. Become aware. Your intuition will guide you through such things.

Some weeks later I was committed to jury service back in New Zealand, and I knew I needed to ask for help. I cycled to the nearby emergency hospital department to seek help. The hospital process is good and I was placed on schedule for open-heart surgery. Good news that I could be mended!

The New Zealand system provides free health care in such situations, and the operation was done in a private hospital by the same surgical staff, as the public facility was too busy, from an increase in heart patients due to post-earthquake disaster stress.

There are a lot of neurons in your heart. A friend who had a heart transplanted into him from a twenty-seven-year-old sportsman who overhydrated and died was sure his consciousness field was still the same. The soul must be a greater field.

There are protocols to this medical procedure. You need faith and belief that the work of the surgeon will go well.

Life has a way of providing challenges. What makes for a good life? Quiet, meditative mindfulness parts to your day, some change in your life, thus adding some creativity to your life as this comes from your intuitive energy and thus allows for new ways of living and getting the best out of life.

If you keep a journal, then that writing is coming from the inner soul.

When you go through an open-heart surgical procedure, your life is very much interfered with: the closing down, cooling of the body, the help of bypass and life being, shall we say, reconstituted. The medical people have good protocols for this work. It is amazing but well-acted throughout the world, in good procedural fashion.

To follow this work, there is healing for your body; it is manageable and life returns. There may be no definite symptom that will alert you of the failing part, nor is there a common set of circumstances for people who undergo this procedure. There can be fibrillation problems as the heart starts retraining. It may be that depressive symptoms and feelings of up and down energy can be experienced. Both are manageable.

When you face such major health events and healing is necessary for survival, the considerations are numerous. Having been alongside the process with a number of people, I have some considered opinions. I'm not sure what the right ways to look at dealing with life-threatening matters is, but surely there are balanced ideas from many people's experiences upon which we can rely.

Medical people have spent a lot of time training, experiencing, and giving guidance to their patients. There is wisdom here and you need to listen. There are quite a number of dimensions in life. A holistic, all-considerations avenue is there for us. Listen to your own energy as well. We have sayings: "we are all one" and "the universe is within you." Unqualified radiance of energy is within and you just need to open to it. As much as this is wordy, it is the first major step toward having intuitive life find you more than you realized. That is the key to your passage.

The surgeon who repaired my heart had me up and walking right away, telling my body to get itself into action, and then to get active, to heal myself—it works. They know this. Take their advice.

CHAPTER 20

UNDERSTANDING MEDICAL
PEOPLE, CONDITIONS,
AND YOURSELF

I have heard people talking about loving their condition. While some people say, they will fight the health problem, others say, "Love your body and all that it entails, and if there is ill performing parts to it, love your being and ask for the non-functioning parts to heal, to remove the illness and allow the body to recuperate."

It's not mystic … yet maybe it is. Maybe you sometimes have to revisit the idea to come to terms with what the interpretation really is. As an example, warts might disappear with such an approach, to love thyself, and better not to suffer the side effects of required medications.

What is clear in this modern age is that people are stressed from daily activities and need calming. Mindfulness is the term we often use, for when people can calm to the inner self. I was on an ECG machine prior to my open-heart procedure and the nurse asked, "What have you been doing since the earthquake?"

I went on to say, "See staff off, fight the insurance companies, deal with the banks, work alongside the tax department, etc."

"Wow, stop," she said. "You're going off the charts."

What I realized was that for a teacher or any person dealing with challenging circumstances, the stress effect is millisecond quick! I don't think people are aware of the speed, and thus, the effect.

Many people are just not connected to strong meditative ways and divert their attention to busy lives.

There are lots of published guides on how to be meditative. A mindful process I use to initiate people into ease response is: Sit on a chair, feet flat and grounded; breathe deep and from your tummy; then work through feeling your feet, legs, pelvis, body, shoulder, arms, hands, neck, face, head, roll it back.

Be calm. You can do it even when doing physical tasks. Just get started.

An electrician I know was working late at my place at the end of a week. I invited him to a glass of red wine. I didn't know he didn't usually drink like that. We talked. He told me of a conflict with a client family who verbally attacked him when told the job perhaps couldn't be finished in the day. The electrician retorted back and was so affected by his loss of control that he drove for some time through the countryside to calm down.

I suggested that in the trueness of the Buddhist saying "When the student is ready, the teacher arrives," he had to be the teacher; they were tense from post-earthquake tension and the difficulties of getting things done.

And that was the case. The electrician came again to my place and alerted to me that he was "doing mindfulness" and that he had discovered that drinking a couple of glasses of red wine in the evening was a great relaxer. Some time on he was proud and confident to say that he was undergoing hypnotherapy and it was very good for him. He's a very good tradesman, boss of his company, and a good operator. Just a little bit of mindfulness, listening to his self, and his life was moving to another level, and so be it for all of us. Calm.

This afternoon I was feeling lost, empty, and I guess you would say sad. That wasn't a usual experience for me. I work from a heightened spiritual awareness and can find positives in a day, even if you have to laugh about fixations you see that people have on less vital life matters. I know that such feelings can be a precursor to less good energy. Sad news, concerns. I so often kick myself if I haven't paid enough respect to having faith and believing. Listen to your emotions, feelings, yourself, your subconscious—call it what you will.

A message came through from friends in another country. There was news, but I didn't know what. He was a young student in my early teaching life, and he has never lost the respect! He is a master. She, his wife, has good self-actual understandings and is able to understand and carry out affirmations for good living. I telephoned Australia and the week would see her daughter married, then she tearfully told me she had throat cancer and had started treatment that morning. I know you would like Wendy. She has a lovely disposition.

I told her of love and good energy to be sent her way. We will all be together with her challenge. What you have read in this chapter I have passed on.

Listen to suggestions of loving and caring for your body to get clear of that, which is a problem.

Listen to and work with the medical staff.

Create a simple mindfulness exercise without complexity. There are lots of published mindfulness activities, or search online. The task of doing even a simple mindful exercise turns the body's focus toward inner life, looking at what goes on within the intuitive body. Hence, calming meditative approaches and mindfulness tasks that focus your thoughts inward are the driver toward being more intuitive. They all work toward the same awareness.

Here is what I told her:

Developments of meditation practices are always possible.
Laugh when you can.
Want and expect your partner, me, your friends and family to

be mindful of your need for good energy support. Good food, good exercise.

Accept the challenge. And go and really enjoy the wedding of your daughter.

She said it was timely and what we talked of was needed.

Is there more than love, goodness, cherishment, and newness of thinking of future life? Relaxation and awareness and increased optimism. Take steps forward for this. We are now looking to use self-actualization, the inward-looking power of self and common sense ideas that your being will accept to improve deeper ways to look at powerful life, that can overcome the negatives that are known to cause ill health. There is a gift from other people in our lives. There are many published ways, techniques, and attitudes that you can use going forward. Be open to them. If it makes more common sense, then it will be more acceptable, a whole new way of seeing things. Adopt it now, and not just after you have a reawakened experience.

Using the ideas and ways and means of living a more intuitive life such as you first read about in chapter 1 can be incorporated into your daily life, and business ways and means can be further based on an intuitive awareness. How about taking the first idea that comes to you and explore it more? We all know our initial thoughts are often the best.

CHAPTER 21

MENTALLY ON EDGE

Life can be a challenge. More so for some people, especially those who are mentally challenged. Finding a recognized normality is not possible. If you haven't met up with someone who falls into this grouping, you will. Life challenges. Depression, hallucinations, manic behavior. You can question yourself, thinking it must be your side of friendships/relationships. When you haven't been able to acknowledge that a person has a condition, it can be one big challenge to you.

Is it that people can't change to a comfort-balanced life? Is it spiritual inner being out of balance? Is the chemistry of the body awry? I have seen ramifications of this when people suddenly act out, throwing all caution to the wind. I have seen people reacting to hallucinations when I don't see what they see! I have known of people committing suicide because of being mentally challenged. Can this be the soulfulness running out? No place to go. Good authors have explained the dark tunnel they have experienced and the challenge to get beyond the fear of that challenge, but for finding a way, they are confident of handling such events. Depression can happen in the day!

How do you know this state of living on the edge? Of somewhat comfortable living, but with emotions that challenge a life. I can tell of depressive behavior that followed having to have open-heart surgery. It is a major procedure for a surgeon and team, and despite the protocols and wonderment of such medical procedures being possible, there is a certain interfering with the mojo of our being. The soulfulness of ourselves does not like being interfered with in this way. The process after is to acknowledge, start a chemical regime to boost the body's needs, and, for me, eventually take a challenge that would in my mind tell my mojo I am okay. I don't know really for sure what that is, but I knew that when I faced a nineteen-foot wave at Honolua Bay, I was in the abyss of whether I could be or not.

The matters that followed the heart operation were a challenge, yet the surfing challenge at Honolua Bay provided an inner recovery. They were all part of my passage. I gained confidence over several days on those Maui waves. Honolua Bay is a famous wave break. The power of the water necessitated a big paddle along the coast, out and back to the point where the wave energy built up. Finally aligned with the swells, I looked sideways to see a surfer in the tube of the wave, standing upright, as if he was holding the wave to the heavens. Not for me, a quick paddle out and then to face the next wave. It was all disaster. Me, scraped on rocks, the board broken into three parts, a challenge to survive, nearly impaled on that rocky abutment that water surges around before moving back out into the bay. But I was intact and my inner being, my mojo, was back. Sometimes being at the edge of the abyss is part of the learning, to move to greater things, discovering "who I am."

Unleashing yourself is a complex and challenging task. There will be many different avenues. For me, it was a surfboard adventure. For the hallucinating woman, it was to disavow those around her and move with two children to who knows where. For the manic guy to accept that exhilarated edge like behavior was scary to acquaintances, and that he and his talented wife and two young boys could get some solace from where their dad was adrift if he was willing to acknowledge his need for mental health care.

Many things that will happen and will trigger how your body and mind react. That's medical. Seek medical help.

What can you do? Listen to music. Connect with other people. Establish a friend as a "therapist." and talk daily to that person. Talk to an actual therapist. Go online for helping services. Relax, exercise at a gym, walk on the beach, get a dog or cat, be mindful and focus on what is going on at that moment. That will focus your thoughts back to yourself, your very *self*. Go green, find a garden or a park space that you can commune in. Massage is nice. Try a holiday in Thailand.

It is about being aware that you are creating your passage in life. Work on it, be open to it.

Can the body be spiritually out of balance? Yes. Can we work on behaviors that challenge us by learning spiritual awareness? Yes. Can we change our spiritual base by changing our spiritual order? Yes! We can change our sentient pathway from what we think will be our life's journey to what becomes our life's journey. Higher orders of spirituality can be developed at many junctions throughout our lives. Whenever we have a quandary or question challenging things, we need to go back to source.

Go to where your inner self is—the spirit, your soul. So here we are now, at the source, and that means looking at our attitudes and feelings. Many just accept that the universe is in you. The important questions you need to ask and the answers that are so important to your personal realm are within you. Go there and deal with your life from that stance. Your passage in life has to be about this openness. So often you hear people say, "I sought answers across the globe, but I found them where I came from."

This is not an intellectual pursuit. It is about openness, so take what you receive from the questions and be empowered by that.

CHAPTER 22

COLLECTIVE POWER/WISDOM

Terrorists attacked America on 911. What are terrorists? And why did they attack?

In work life, bosses who have a sterling philosophy know there is more to focus on than the bottom line, that success and profit come from collective force, from workers joining together, and that timing and luck have much to do with the direction and value that a business is able to achieve. Intuition is certainly a power force to those who start up and drive new realms of entrepreneurial endeavors.

If you look for power forces that drive organizational acumen, the teenage years is a good place to start. Parents may be the precursors of direction of a young person's life. Peer groups become all powerful as the years go by. Sometimes youth cells of collective sameness behavior can lead to panic and despair. The results can be shocking. With this in mind it is the collective cell that successfully created havoc with the destruction of the World Trade Center towers. Horror success!

I was at a friend's wedding in New Orleans. The next day we were sitting around on the floor of the suite of the wedding couple, Adam and Amanda. New York based, they chose New Orleans as the place for their friends to gather for this occasion. We mused that despite the media view that a lot of things made for a supposed great life, it was collective relationships, togetherness, that was all powerful. Like sitting around on the hotel room floor. Schmoozing, but powerfully schmoozing. Hanging about.

The Hamburg cell of young men was too, and by luck they carried out their destructive efforts on 911.

I was in Washington, DC having lunch with a bunch of ex CIA personnel who had left that organization over a variety of political issues of the time, including the Valerie Plame affair, where undercover agent Plame was outed by journalist Robert Novak.

The world saw quite a few terrorist attacks where small groups were active. I suggested that like the teenage cell's intrinsic power, the terrorist group was also profoundly built from within. It may have suited politicians to focus people on saying, "You are either for us or against us," but really, that was more about pushing countries to join military efforts rather than a real understanding of the global situation. The ex CIA officers gathered concurred.

The ISIS uprising as a caliphate is a mixture of young people, some disparate participants from other countries around the world, yet they are clearly pitting themselves against the other Iran-based side. Such a pity that the power within younger people's ranks is lost in a world that could use such skills if productively used to address the needs of humanity. But they want recognition.

The great Indian teacher Jiddu Krishnamurti spoke of the inner awareness of understanding the source of peacefulness in our being, and he said that until leaders learned that going to Source is the answer, the peaceful resolution of world conflicts would remain unresolved. What happens now is a kind of junior management as they sort out some curtailment of force as the best that will be done. The answer is in all of us! In Source. The answers lie within us. Tune in to your intuition. This is how you will better understand the bigger issues that have led to a disordered global situation. Above all, a better understanding of what is peace can be realized for us.

The elements of a successful unified workforce are also open to collective power generated not just from the top. Knowing the janitors may or may not change the institution or the ways of going ahead with the organizational work will certainly tell you something of the nature of the person who wields the power and how he or she sees the model of the organization the person heads.

At the high school where I taught, there was wisdom in the saying that "the staff who drinks together works together". It worked. It was a well-oiled machine! It worked well, by a cohesive teaching staff. Time changed that as we became more aware of what our drinking and driving obligations were, but elements are still there that I don't see in all other institutions. Choose wisely, I say. Look for humor too, as a reflection that a staff that plays together will be the good one to work with.

It is clear from recent terrorism activity in Paris and Belgium that small groups operate to carry out these acts, but there are much grander organized forces at bay.

Social media is used powerfully. Information reaches far. Good media can cover actions in depth. But as my friend Danny Murray reminds me, the Fourth Estate (which is defined as a societal or political force or institution whose influence is not consistently or officially recognized. It most commonly refers to the news media, especially print journalism) "can be an inch deep and spread widely as technology has allowed truth to be spread without any rational thought." People are more afraid, and governments use that to bolster their support.

Understanding needs to come from intuitive reference, answering the big questions. The real answers come from within. We all need peace. I have found that the greater answers have come from the understanding we have developed within ourselves. This adds to intuitive life, the understanding of what is part of our being.

CHAPTER 23

HOW TO BE BAD

Intuitive energy comes from inner understanding, such as knowing before you know. To really latch on to the power force of being, go with nature, the sun. It is the shining energy within all people. It doesn't choose. Use nature as your guide, and you will know the divine. You will find ecstasy in the natural world, and that is beauty.

When this all goes to waste, what is the "badness factor"? Reflection and integrity are parts of the order of true being. When you have a bigger picture of your true self, you will be spiritually enlightened in day-to-day living. There are always some downfalls, but there is a balance toward goodness.

When skills or circumstance reduce the options to be reflective before active behavior, and to be led astray by false elements of life (such as the misuse of money), then you can have misbehavior. Lack of self-control. Is bad behavior wicked? Is it evil? To a teacher, a student can be badly behaved. What was it about? We could explain it as being caused by something else, but that doesn't excuse it. Complicated, isn't it?

We can agree that it is not enjoyable to have to experience people's bad behavior, which doesn't meet some standard of general acceptance. What is bad behavior though? When does sexual behavior change from being seen as good to being bad?

Can we say that some people just screw up from having

misplaced values and that they lose touch with their innate inner freedom? Their values become pretty false. I don't think they have a sense of reflecting on intuitive knowing. When I meet and relate to someone who is what I call spiritual, there is no argument between us. You cannot argue with that person. The opposing forces have been balanced. That is a nice thing. When forces of yin and yang are not balanced, there is difficulty in the relationship.

You are free to make decisions, and you will have consequences. The rub comes when the choices are not amenable to good decision making and results in bad decisions. Is it because people deceive themselves?

CHAPTER 24

WHAT'S IT ALL TELLING YOU?

You can love people, places, and things. When all these become one in happiness, that is love.

You have to change things.

Nature is breathable. Oceans, forests, your food garden—love them all.

Do you know people with whom you can grow? Find good friends.

Get where you need to go when it is time to be there. Not one moment sooner. Then relax, breathe.

Keep something in store, and never speak everything you know.

It's about appreciating and not gathering belongings. Have extravagance in your place. See nice things in small appreciations.

I have a simple garden. The roses are always a challenge and blooms are treasured. Yesterday I heard the very sweet sounds, a heavenly sweetness, of a bellbird. There were other birds in the same tree. I have lots of trees for birds. I take down trees at some stage, mourn their loss, but always replant more. Such is it for urban tree life and the birds.

As you sort out your life, as we all do, you will need to balance between your comfort level and risk-taking. This can be by intuitive energy. How will you be different by focusing on your intuition? You will know your partner's real feelings. You will have a better sense of who to avoid so you can surround yourself with more positive people. People come alive when they can break out of cognitive illusions of false messages that your ego mind has been leading you on. That can be quite a revelation.

I have found that working at a higher spiritual level takes you away from so much of the petty drivel that takes up life from day to day—getting consent, asking for information about an area you want help with. Daily grind! How so often it is of people working on their own platform, while they cover their backs. It's excruciating to a creative, entrepreneurial, excited mind.

When you get to talk with another person who understands heightened spiritual life, you find calmness and understanding. It is empowering and peaceful, filled with learning and growth. It is good to work with and practice having a better use of spiritual life.

People with a sixth sense, high self-intuitive energy can be helpful in communicating the intuitiveness of others.

The opposite can occur when you have feelings that bring anxiety.

Into the pure is when you feel like your thoughts are clear like water. Into the pure is making sense in the right place.

We had another earthquake that registered 4.7 on the Richter scale just earlier as I was writing this. Quite a rugged shake that sent the building swaying. Most of the earthquakes through the major period of disaster for Christchurch, New Zealand were between September 2010 and June 2011.

I was on my way from the Les Mills Gym back to my New York Soho West Village styled hotel called Off the Square. The local TV station CTV was alongside the gym. I had to divert from the more direct walk along Manchester Street that was barricaded off due to danger from collapsing buildings from earlier earthquakes. I stopped outside the entrance to the CTV reception. It was closed and dark. I knew this company and the work they did. There was an international school operating in part of the CTV building. I don't know why I was fixated with standing there for twenty seconds or more.

The next afternoon at 12:51 the most disastrous quake happened, from three miles below the city. One hundred twelve people were killed in this building when it collapsed. Sadly, many young Japanese students were among them.

I was nearby leading hotel guests and staff from the downtown area of our city. We housed many of them some distance out at Lincoln in the countryside, where there were fewer shockwaves. Nevertheless, the earthquakes still rumbled through the night. Was it premonition that this coincidence occurred? We can't know, as these things are not explainable. When we look back, reasons for our behavior become better understood.

I was clearly involved and affected by the earthquake disaster. It is a passing that leaves room for immense change in your inner being. You just have to get on, but not without many differences now. Our inner realm is very much being challenged.

As an aside, I have been thinking that coincidental angles, from when I was doing geometry at our small grammar school, were identical angles. Perfect fit. Coincidence is not a "just happened by chance" occurrence! We should consider a different perspective from these occasions than the ones commonly thought of.

Those who want to turn away from opening to intuitive life are opening to worry and fear. They lose out on not being aware. In the naturalness of intuitive life, it can be thought of as information gathered that hasn't been put into words but is held in your subconscious. It doesn't have to take over your life. Use it as part of your decision making of daily management. Powerful forces with just some people, our unique leaders, should be seen as a blessing to them, albeit a challenge for that person. They have things to teach. Could be spiritually guided people from many walks of life. There are some amazing musicians with unique stories to tell through their music. So, if singing is the answer to intuitive sense and spiritual life, sing!

Welcome the gift. Is it a mystery?

Ignore people who get in the way of your dreams, creativity, visions, and inspiration. Change is always necessary and often good. Find life! Don't tell people what you think they should hear unless they have asked you to. You and they should reject unsolicited advice. It will be about their and your best interests.

Through tragic and wonderful events, what happens for you is for you. I feel that we are dealing in human energy, and I don't see how matters of chance fit into this, but maybe if you enter into your subconscious a message of winning the lottery, you will certainly know before you know when the numbers come up! I think it would be very unexpected chance.

Let intuition be your mainstay, the most useful and unused sense. I see it as a sacred gift.

Movies will reveal something early in the plot to hook us into what is coming later. Intuition hooks us into the journey we are on. The intuitive energy will be there and then not there, but you can call on it. It's a flash of knowing in an instant.

If you sit on a beach watching the sunset, you might just see the flash that lasts for a second or two. It is the sun changing color, a green spot on the remaining disk of the sun, often seen by airline pilots flying westward. Fun!

Think of it like the flash of intuition. Don't fear the power of things revealed and the transforming power of what will follow. It is of nature, and it is for the better.

CHAPTER 25

Finding the Intuitive Realm

Before you hear of more adventures and travel on our globe, let's give thought to how it works.

Be open to finding more from within. Don't ignore intuitive power just because it happens so naturally and is not always obvious. If you are open to it, it will find you.

There is a Buddhist saying: when the student is ready, the teacher arrives. That teacher could be a person you just wanted to get to know.

If you want to understand why you live, what your place in the world is all about, then get intuitive.

Write some carefully crafted questions on paper, what is driving your needs. Wait, and you will be answered.

People who become misinformed and get scammed are not listening well to their inner guides.

We all want peace when there has been chaos, as we do at the end of a work week when we seek relaxation.

If you get into difficult situations, trust your intuition. Don't analyzes yourself into paralysis. Instinct and intuition will rule the day.

Like the universe, intuition is in you, and all of the way is in us.

Don't seek the answers elsewhere. That's why the questions you ask of yourself will be the most important ones you will ever answer.

You can work toward being in touch with communications from your inner self. You can seek guidance on that.

Streaming thought can be like teaching. You discuss the matter at hand, and then you should go away and write down what was said. Then get the original purveyor of the information to read and cover what was meant to be the understandings, now noting where this hadn't clearly gotten through.

This provides a double consideration of the learning and sorts out any confusion. This would be pretty typical of a school classroom, yet would be more individually focused in a discussion with, say, a doctor.

How do you reach the inner part of self about these such considerations? What is inner meaningfulness when you need to call on it? That should be done daily. There is a source of energy you can draw on. You won't fully meet that need with food and drink. This is the inner being energy. You will know it as spirit. In China it is referred to as chi and is available to those who are open to it, and then a whole greater sense of empowerment is for you. It will rub off on people, and what is exciting is that you learn new things. You will not find a need to close off to life's offerings. You are becoming a better self-actualized person.

CHAPTER 26

THE EDGE IS GOOD FOR YOU

What is your comfort level in relation to risk taking? Use your intuition here. If it feels right, you have an answer. Be conscious and reactive to the additional things that can make your life better. The energy of life that will help you with this, the real life, never changes. It is the divine peace side of your life and will give you as perfect an infinite life as you can get. You are looking for the extraordinary while you carry out the ordinary. Defer to the inside self, which is timeless consciousness. If you are well tuned to this, you will drive out any false sense of self that may inhabit your thinking. You need to feed your soul because it is larger than yourself.

You are the custodian of your own world. I see avenues for seeking the edge of what is ahead of you. The edge is where the sedentary non-change meets change. If we see that change and how we react to it is vital to managing your life well, it is a major element in how well we live life…

Edge behavior and form that instigates change are at the forefront of a trend, when it is experimental or avant-garde. It is bold, provocative, or of unconventional quality. The edge concept is where change influences impose differences to the rest of a group. New York is really exemplar of where such change is always occurring. It's further to the concept of where species change more so at the edge where the species meet and interact. It's the universal nature of change.

I am often in New York City, around Washington Square Park at the southern end of Fifth Avenue. The park is central to New York University. It is an intersection of people. There is a tiered down inward circle of steps. You are part of a cavalcade of colorful combatants. People on display seem to say "watch me in a bikini" or "see me skate by." Some people will push the envelope of what normally happens at public gatherings. Others will just gravitate along with the process.

We see changes in biological cell processes when the organism comes into contact with other forces, such that species change. The members of a species most unaffected by change will be buried inward in a comfort zone, with less contact.

New York is like that. City areas are always undergoing transition, and suddenly you have newness, the next big thing.

It is good to live afar, travel, and absorb difference. Learn the change that comes from these times. Sometimes we have to travel to away places to find peace. Maybe peace will come from whence you came: home. All these aspects are vital to finding your passage in life as is intuitive understanding and learning within that.

I had the experience of creating, designing, and operating the Off the Square Hotel in Christchurch, New Zealand. After it was established, I realized it reflected the development of boutique hotels in New York. In a more modern time it was certainly something akin to the famous heritage Chelsea Hotel in New York. I made it a point to travel there quite regularly and spent a good amount of time exploring the unique boutique hotel. I came up with a list, and after comparing notes with Chip Conley, who runs the Joie de Vivre boutique hotels in San Francisco, we agreed on the same list. This was part of my passage, of determining the driving forces in the creative processes behind boutique hotels in New York.

New York has always been vital to my passage.

We all have journeys in us.

CHAPTER 27

POC DUDES

Out of a London pub gathering, it was determined that several hundred internationally related associates would gather for a party of the century (POC) on Pangkor Laut Island in Malaysia. Pavarotti, the famed Italian opera singer, called the place "heaven on earth."

We managed through the years to keep feeding a London bank account, and it came time to spend a week around the dawning of a new century.

It is remarkable when someone can lead, create the energy, and hold that together over such a period of time. It has to be seen as more than just organizing. Our man at the helm was Tony Stuart, once in charge of British Airways and manager of Manchester Airport, later manager of Sydney Airport through the 2000 Olympics.

What drives an occasion like this? Tony, really. A man who has zeal to attract and facilitate good friendships between like-minded people. Who came? Two hundred sixty-five open and versatile people from all continents.

When we had New Year celebrations for the year 2000, there were Kiwis, Aussies, Malaysians, people from Singapore, the Middle East, Paris, London, New York City, Colorado, Los Angeles, and Hawaii celebrating the big occasion. The Hawaiian host was a surf competition promoter. I remember saying no to his generous offer to come have some champagne! Despite being the winner of a bottle of Dom from earlier in the week from wearing pretty skimpy garb at the toga party, when I attempted a "share with me" get-together to drink it when back in Kuala Lumpur, there were no takers. Champagne had become passé!

Cool event, yet there was more to it than just logistics. There were people who passed out of the network during the lead-up time, and children came into the picture. There was no place for additions unless from these two ways. I remember a sense of "we did it," a sure sense of overdoing it on celebration, a sense of "these could be some best times" (and watch out for monkey intruders from the forest!). There were a bunch of great beach areas, one considered one of the best beaches in the world. Yes, it was memorable. The photographs were great. All cool!

We all need change and celebration in our lives, and mojo matters. The inner sense of being with difference is spiritual divinity. This was a great event, as much in the doing as in the culmination. The new century dawned cloudy and dull. The feelings were good though. Travel is needed to address these fulfillments.

From Pangkor Laut I was due in Mumbai. The flight arrived at 2:30 a.m. during a taxi strike. On leaving the terminal into sultry air, there was no obvious way to handle getting to some accommodation. I wandered about until I came across a blind boy who, for a coin, enabled a call on a phone that was passed through a small hole in the wall. Waiting for a long time with my backpack for someone to pick me up—this blonde-haired, lean, tan and white shirted traveler was quite a sight for the hundreds of Indian boys hanging around. I was unsure about things, and the transport through dark, smoky streets added to the uneasy feeling. When I was in a room with barred windows but no lock, I felt even more uneasy. I fastened and locked my pack to furniture and sort of slept.

The next day I noticed a Hindu temple outside. Life brought about a sense of warmth, and India might have been starting to show its raison d'etre. Of course, it was to be a grand time visiting Mumbai, Goa, Nagpur, and Delhi with some super friends from around the world. India might challenge but doesn't disappoint. It can frustrate, but it adds wonder. It can seem wrong, but then it comes by all right. It's the spiritual nature of the place. They have had some practice!

My international friends and I had been involved with Samaritan healing work in Turkey. I had picked up a stomach bug and had failed over many weeks to get rid of it. On returning to New Zealand, I had rapid medical intervention, as they suspected cholera or something wild! It was a complex B staph infection, and on perusing a drug list (one said it was not to be used if fathering a child in the next six months), I began a course of pills.

Four days later I felt at ease as my body could give up trying to fight the bug by itself. Relief. I decided that if I was ever again to be faced with such a malady, I would immediately seek help back home or head for London!

From Kuala Lumpur, many of our group picked up an alimentary canal bug, and I felt that heading into India would be a challenge. I thought I would give it four days, and if it continued, I would set travel aside to seek help.

On the fourth day I arrived in Mumbai, and by the next day the symptoms were gone. Relief. India, here we come.

I accept that help can be found in most places in this world, but if persistence occurs, think wisely.

These are all part of the experiences of traveling to new places. Go to mystic levels, when all great earthly energies come together, and you will be a smug bunny in a world of great traverses, of great inner energy.

Your spiritual passage is going to be enhanced by stepping out and stretching the dimensions of life.

Joy Nicholls

Tim Zen of Life

Passage and vision to the future

Blackie cat

Poppy and Snuky

EQ Chairs   Tim at Indian Festival

Timmy at 16 years   Surfing Honolua Bay

Tim in Melbourne

CHAPTER 28

SERMON ON THE MOUNT

What would you say in your last gasp of breath? What words of wisdom would you leave for others?

The late Dr. Wayne Dyer was asked to give his sermon on the mount. The day before his passing, he talked publicly of his excitement, humility, and enthusiasm for what was to come in carrying this out. His sermon-like lecture has been repeated many times, since he gave such a new brushstroke of what could be in the field of personal development. Think about how we can self-actualize our behavior and do so in a nondenominational spiritual realm.

Can you not get excited about finding more within yourself than you knew was there? Pessimism must be worked out, and the limits you impose on yourself have to be expanded. Just muse on it. Put on your hat and suspenders, curl up, shake your hair a bit, and chat with someone on a spiritual plane that you can relate to. See where that takes you.

I used to be unnerved by the stark glare of a full moon night. Now I love the energy of a warm moonlit night, beautiful moonlit mind. What changed? Maybe from when I was myself, my body, but now I am the universe in my body. This new self-realization is about getting away from the attachment we have with our own identities—being the ego—which Dr. Dyer called edging God out, or EGO.

"What's My Sermon?"
Be one with all.
Deal with the moment.
Befriend the self.
Find the least painful way to move forward.

You don't have to reach heights. You don't need to find a way that goes between challenges; you just have to be in self to hear the best for you.

Don't go the way of wanting to control all matters, all things. That's arrogance. Calm and tread in friendship with yourself. Then you will want to do more and will have realness in your life.

Be with people and hear what they're saying. They don't want answers, just acknowledgement. They, like we, have to befriend themselves, so listen to the messengers of our self-energy. Be bountiful with yourself, and that will reflect on the world around you. Could it be a Large Hadron Collider resonance?

Accepting the passage of age will give you energy to live a born-again experience. A kind of immortality. Now we see beauty and sense that goodwill from us will bring good energy in return.

I like the Buddhist saying, "When the student is ready, the teacher arrives." A new animal friend might just walk into your life. Keep your eyes open.

Perhaps chat with a Buddhist follower, or a spiritual connector spirit reader, a person who has mastered anything well (such as a great gardener), but work with yourself, because the universe is all truly in there.

Can the following be what the actual sermon on the mount (Jesus's lecture) was about?

- You can be without material wealth, but you can still have all the power of the universe.
- When you feel sad, be comforted that the world has a place for all things.

- Humility will win through. Be quiet to the turmoil of the earth. You will find peace.
- Feel for what is right in this life. You will be supported.
- Give mercifulness as we will receive mercifulness in return.
- Be of good heart. A fine person. You will see God.
- Those who seek peace will be those acknowledged as the sons of God.
- Those who are righteous, but persecuted, will be honored.
- Be blessed that for all that is difficult in your life, you can be rewarded. Have faith.

Dr. Dyer spoke of receiving the messages that came by to his hand for him to record. I certainly feel that this book has come from the same passageway, and my version of a sermon on the mount is again receiving and passing on the ideas that I have written above. It comes from the intuition. This is where answers, ideas, concepts, understandings, creative forms, and much more come from.

CHAPTER 29

SPORTS—WHAT MAKES A GREAT PERFORMANCE?

Kobe Bryant retired with a massive following. In China, he is known from TV commercials. He visits each year and learned to speak some Mandarin. His golden times have been from a long history of high-level performances, hard work, and perseverance. There's magic in the air!

Sports thrills, and it provides unique experiences for athletes and their supporters. When we see an athlete winning gold at the Olympics, we marvel at the high level of performance. How does the athlete validate this performance? How is it carried out? Often there is a long preparation with less successful results. You can follow performances that have been disappointing, especially when the athlete is new to the world of competition. Top-level competitions in earlier times were made by making selection for a national team.

Given time to prepare when the thirst to succeed is internally validated, you can expect success, enhanced by the spirit of time and place of an Olympic event. Prime competitors have repeated their skills many times, and from the subconscious store of wise knowledge comes the base for great performance. But great success needs to come from a higher level. This is the inner drive.

A relative of mine created a Nike project to film footage of an outstanding Kobe Bryant basketball game. Separate footage of a set-up audience was filmed. Hundreds of LED screens were placed around the court. A person could be filmed moving to various spots and then magically interposed with the other film to create an event where the guest becomes central to the play and player. Wow. I think a whole bunch of CEOs were keen to participate in that. Thus, with virtual reality and augmented reality adjustments, the sport is a hybrid between real and created.

Another friend whose son became a San Francisco Forty-Niner, with three Super Bowls under his belt in a decade, was from New Zealand and had a native Maori background and private New Zealand Presbyterian schooling. Being on that famous NFL team had to have something to do with his background but also with his mother's move to the United States. The son's son has now become a starting player with the Vikings.

Sometimes the success is even more impressive, as when I watched track athlete Australian John Steffenson, a 4 x 400 meter relay silver medalist, at the 2004 Olympics. He was the golden boy who was expected to succeed at the Melbourne Commonwealth games. What pressure and what a win in the 400 meter final. Athens magic!

I was at a previous Commonwealth Games in Edmonton when Rod Dixon, one of the great middle distance runners and New York marathon winner, was in the 5,000 meter final. He didn't appear on the track at the line-up. A Canadian friend working in the competitors' warm-up area suddenly came running toward our stand. What was up? His gear bag containing his track shoes had been placed behind a tree and was momentarily lost. We rustled up a pair of spikes, and Rod made it to the starting line with two minutes to spare.

I was in the competitors' area at the swimming pool at the same games when an English athlete sat down beside me, and we had a great discussion. I had been a competitive swimmer. I didn't know his fame. Yes, he was an athlete. The next day I was to see him enter the arena to compete in the decathlon. Yes, he was the famous young British decathlete Daley Thompson, who set the world alight.

I watched as he left the competitor line to shake hands with all the officials, and then the fire of the competition was on.

A super example of success is the New Zealand All Blacks rugby team, which won the four-yearly world cup in London in 2015. That was two world championships in a row. That national team has been the most successful at such high levels over a century that the record stands in the world. I was a rugby referee for more than eleven years and our play in the region was staunch and often quite droll. The world of sports has changed a great deal, and the All Blacks (known for their black uniforms and their native Maori Haka war chant) were a far different team from anything in the past. They were living with a touched attitude. Know yourself, know your skill requirement. Know your part on the team. Know how to connect with the media. Know how to connect to the greater community, schools, and the like. Then and above all, prepare, prepare, and prepare. There is a Maori saying: "What is important? It is people, it is people, it is people!" "Kia Kaha"—be strong! And that they were.

Dan Carter was a member of that team, the awardee of honor of being the greatest rugby player in the world and at the 2016 world championship event, particularly the final—he was outshining anything. As an observer, the culmination of all of these factors leaves one in tears, for it is more whole, truly so, than the sum of the parts, and it is truly to that that classic heights were achieved.

How does Dan Carter, famous also for advertising Jockey underwear, among other things, put together such a spectacular performance? Through years and years of skill, practice, playing, and ups and downs. The injuries and the sad and tough times. What is true is that the skill level has been so deeply immersed into his subconscious that a reaction to kick and send play in a particular direction is instantaneous and makes for great depths of considered playing, but deep in the vault of a life. You get something from work—conditioning, considerations on the surface level—yet beyond his stunning skill you see the greatness emerge, and that it did. That's how we have our super athletes! It's intuition.

This is the culmination that makes for good sport. That which draws the supporter to many events. Love it, some say. It is an inner-self-connected attribute, and focus on understanding self will overcome. The voice of ego to worldly considerations is what we read about, as the fame of sportspeople is then unmanageable, and they let themselves down.

The golfing world seems to have a startling number of young players coming through. When skills are demonstrated, and then even more, we should look to an uncluttered outer ego voice that enhances the mojo. Youth seems better able to focus on inner zones of balance, reflection, and mindful calmness. Is there any other way of looking at these global results?

Validating performance in sport is the same as validating your business proposal. Who, what, when, where, and why—the old journalist's lexicon—need to be sorted. In a recent book in which I contributed, I explained the validation of businesses looking for foolproof ways to increase business and make it happen.

Like the importance of luck and timing in business, there is also an element of that in winning Olympic gold. The athlete preparation and knowing oneself will lend to the experience. Big success comes from the inner being. It is about intuition. It is "in the zone."

Sport success is not as simple, or perhaps as complicated, as we want to make it out to be. From training long hours as an Ironman triathlete, I found it was as good to take a piece of your favorite fruit rather than a lot of sticky tube performance enhancers. World surfer Clay Marzo would be out on his board up to ten hours at a time, but the ocean was his place, and it superseded all that was around him, because that wasn't as important.

I have gravitated as a lifestyle free surfer to better understand the grandeur of those who, on flimsy boards, partake in giant ocean energy. They are super beings, and you need to take another look at that, no matter what their level of participation.

Clay Marzo is in a place that others can't go. There is nothing ordinary about what he does. He comes from an Asperger's place and is very separate from normal experiences. He has an inner desire to validate the challenges riding the waves, such that he is able to "rubber band" performance in a way that many see him as the best surfer in the world.

These experiences of Clay's are the process of reaching the inner soul. Each element of being a surfer adds another element of "now," where you're being with nature's energy as it flows right through you. If you don't go there on ocean waves and challenge your mojo, you won't know it, as Clay Marzo knows it.

But there are many other ways that you can reach an exalted life of inner empowerment through sports and exercise. Positivity and openness will do it for you, but we all know people who close off to these enduring energy moments of a life. That negativity is what we often refer to as a half-empty glass.

The self is not just an inner thing. It monitors inner and outer life. When you get the energy of life to meet up with conscious attitudes, and you get the conscious attitudes to meet up with inner life, then your chi is going to be pretty, and with preparation and timing, success rewarded by an Olympic gold is the great fulcrum of all good athletic things. We love that! The inner being of self is benefited by how you have focused your consciousness.

Pay attention. Be open to and experience new realms. If they don't come to you, the great expanse of inner being seems a faraway thing; just think about it. How did the gold performance happen? How did you feel so good about it? We need these things to consider. From this will be the openness you need to receive the feelings that will help identify better with inner self.

The Chinese have the Tao, the centuries of working out how best to live. Here the forces balance with yin and yang, canceling out opposing forces, so you balance sex, food, getting on with people, exercise, and so on. Want to know about a balance of all these forces? Go surfing or sailing!

I truly feel that what enables inner validation to drive performance is intuitive energy, which provides for the great performance that we see, such as achieving Olympic gold.

CHAPTER 30

SPORTS COMMENTS AND GRAND ELEMENTS

Are sports about development and peace? Fitness comes from passion, action, and change. Retrain your body and reformat the mind!

There are certain traditions, and sports can be competitive. Sports can retrain disadvantaged and handicapped people. It is about rules. It provides social structure. You need to be a good sport. It is symbolically about play. There is proper behavior! It's spectacle, shared experience, and magic, seeing what others don't see. it comes from the insight from preparedness, the subconscious preparation, and the intuition to read the play and know what is required before you know it!

Comments regarding sports I have tried:

- Swimming—purist body dynamics to fluvial flow. It's stunning to see records constantly being broken.
- Triathlon—lots of gear, great families, really balanced young people.
- Water polo—you have to be strong in the legs to elevate yourself up, strong in the shoulders, and be able to handle body contact. Can be a rough game. And then you have to swim fast. Strong and skilled young people compete.

- Cycling—oh to be the slimmest and lightest. Big lungs, and strength in legs. Always need to watch out for cars. Look for the driver's eyeballs and where their car wheels are going! If you aren't connecting, you could be in trouble. Everyone falls sometime. Ouch!

- Rugby—running/passing game. Needs smarts of how to play to interpreted rules. Still takes an acute brain to work out the finer points—no trouble makers needed. Works well for certain cultures and university campus sports, especially so for woman at US colleges.

- Rugby sevens—talent on and off the field. Makes for a great day's entertainment, as you get energized by an energetic crowd. A great, continuous spectacle of action.

- Mountaineering—some pain of long days on the move, needs a certain sense of crazy humor and dogged intentions. A kind of culture unto itself!

- Surfing—with skill, talent, lithesome body attributes, good looks, and suntanned body, isn't this the great one? Photo shoots are so often spectacular and these are gods of a sort, more so than most sports. To the less skilled, bumming along on a surf board to the beat of the ocean, salt in your hair in a big scale environment, still equates to a dandy of a time.

- Basketball—a great sport to play. Fitness and skill and off-court play ... for me as a youngster, probably the most enjoyable of all sports I played.

- Olympic athletics—equates to what the Romans did. This is the grand theatre of prime physical exertion. You can't slack off, as everybody is watching. Great drama can unfold at any moment, and when you win well, you win big—just you, on top of the world.

- Sailing—For me, sailing, whether in a small dinghy, or on a fourteen-foot catamaran, or on a yacht, or on a big ocean-going eighty-plus footers—I have been on them all.

Great learning experience being on the water, whether wet and with the elements, or warm and dry while wearing a nice soft rubber dry suit. We used to wear woolly jerseys, up to three layers of them, but we were warm. The speed of a multi-hull yacht is exhilarating and big on spills. Ocean racing is another world of full-on survival, icebergs and all. I still savor memories of the evening drinks on a boat on the Turkish Sea coast.

- Cycling—Best three-day adventure I can remember was in New York. Over the Brooklyn bridge at night, on a 911 anniversary, with two big groupings of lights in the sky. Stopped off at the Kiwi pub Nelson Blue just off the Brooklyn Bridge, then cycled to the meatpacking district, up the west side, down through Central Park. It was raining, and jeans were too tight when they got wet. John Lennon's Strawberry Fields in Central Park is always good to visit, and riding through Times Square at night is sublime. To help, the city has put bike lanes along Third Avenue to go with the traffic flow, but watch out for pedestrians! Phew … but it's good.

- Marathon— A hard grind, but achievement stuff. You have to finish. I learned in an Ironman triathlon that if you run the race in one-mile bits, you eventually get to twenty-six miles. It's in the mind.

- Boxing—love to hate it, but watch it. What's that all about? A good body getting beaten up, even the brain!

This is an off-the-hip list that likely bears no resemblance to how other people find these sports, but there is a grand additional element that is not just body conditioning, and that is the magnificent zen of such activity. I will call it Z for sleep (you need it), E for energy (take along your favorite energy bar and water), and N for "nothing else I want to do in life"—especially if I can get paid to do it! Like the Ironman training, with sports you get to know about yourself in a big way, and that is where the inner being very much comes into it. It will always involve your intuition. It is an intuitive journey!

I was a coach and manager of water polo and triathlon teams. Coaching is a very particular set of skill attributes that enable you to give technical skill advice while promoting a good combination of sportsmanship attributes. Management has to provide for that and all three apex points of the triangle (management, technical, and promotion) have to be included. If the detail is done prior to travel, then it is possible to overcome problems that arise. Unprepared is asking for trouble. Things can and will go wrong.

I was team manager of the New Zealand Women's Water Polo team that played for the Fina World Cup in Los Angeles in 1984. This dovetailed into the Olympics in which the men played. We moved for women's entry to Olympic water polo, but it took another sixteen years to get there. We stopped in Hawaii en route to train at Punahou High School. We were overseas for five weeks, a young male coach and manager and a team of individually strong and of good character Kiwi women.

Three days out from our World Cup we had news of the death of the father of twin sisters on the team. The father was an accomplished water polo referee. We didn't have a great World Cup, but the attitude of team and players to the task at hand was really something. This is an actual accomplishment of a different kind to success, but success in itself. The twins stayed with the team to enable a full complement of players, and the time together was successful.

Some periods of life are all about trial and preparation. These downtimes are necessary to lead to times of great pleasure. Lows to highs. Yin and yang. And that is life. Some of the women water polo players traveled on to Europe for extended overseas travel. This is somewhat traditional among young New Zealanders due to our location as an edge society to the world. United States people were surprised that young people would stay away from their home country for some years. Around one fifth of New Zealanders are in a diaspora around the globe.

Sports encourage diaspora. It's a global business, but it is intuitive, so you just know it's good. Again, my passage was very connected to sporting endeavors. From this I take many understandings, and these experiences eventually provide a springboard for another life more intuitive.

CHAPTER 31

NEITHER LIME NOR LEMON

I like lime, but lemon is good too. A touch of lime juice in water sets things alight. There are commonalities that tie great things together. Music is larger than life and from which we get identity and power.

The late singer Prince said, "All music is inspirational. Let your gift be guided by something more clear!" Be guided by the purity of it. Go to Source, a truly great energy of self, your intuitive realm. That's where all great music comes from. Just study the creative realm of music makers and all becomes clear.

Purple Rain, the movie that set Prince on the way to fame, was released in 1984. I was in Seattle those days, and it was shown at one of those varsity cinemas a little way up on University Way, just by Washington State University.

Jimmy Hendrix was a Seattle boy out of Garfield High School, and he came up with the song "Purple Haze." I was visiting the school once and sat in on an AP physics class. Wandering about, I discovered the school band and realized they were in purple uniforms.

In 2015 I was able to connect with Dr. Wayne Dyer in Auckland, New Zealand, a day before his passing. His signature on his biography had to be in purple, as that was what he wrote his famed forty-three original manuscripts with. More than purple haze, more to the pure, yet these were all truly of the inner spirit. These are men of self.

I grew up in younger days in New Zealand. Part of the British Commonwealth, and while NZ is steadfast and independent, it still has a system of government with the British Queen as Head of State via a New Zealand Governor General. All environs shape our own connectedness with the earth and our being. Geographers know that the landscape reflects our endeavors, yet our lives are reflective of the earth we are anchored are to. So be it that country to country, history will show the difference.

All people are alike but with inbuilt varieties. Speaking out came to be respected in free society, but further back in history the action could get you charged with sedition. There was a drive for music that would provide unison, and music became metaphor for many things. We like to sing together at proms, rock concerts ...

In ancient England, the William Blake poem was to become known as the song "Jerusalem," the apocryphal story of Jesus as a young man wanting to establish the New Jerusalem of universal love and peace.

"And did those feet in ancient time, walk on England's mountains green." God's pastures. There was concern about the "satanic mills," the Industrial Revolution of England that was damaging the nature of human communities. What Blake was on about was the resonance about the repressiveness of this process, weakening society structure.

When students sing "Jerusalem" in school assemblies, it stirs the abstract notion that an invisible and subconscious force is within our outer person. From the Blake poem, we are told to "Bring me my Bow of burning gold; bring me my Arrows of desire: bring me my Spear: O clouds unfold! Bring me my Chariot of fire!" This was acknowledging inner spirit. Jerusalem was a metaphor for heaven, where there would be universal contentment. Peace.

We organized a group of really skilled and talented teenagers to travel to the United States from New Zealand, to perform as part of a 150th anniversary of diplomatic relations between the two countries. It was an opportunity that we grasped with a fine group of high school age youngsters. They all have done well.

George Harrison's versions of "My Sweet Lord" and "While My Guitar Gently Weeps" are stunning. He was the focus of the movie *George Harrison: Living in the Material World*, directed by Martin Scorsese.

Lead guitarist of the Beatles, Harrison followed a journey beyond other musicians. He was the balance between the material world we live in and the serenity we seek. Deep spirituality and humanity are keystones of what he chose, or was open to receive as guides in his life. The movie is a good watch and a super experience of the young Beatles, their co-joined talents, and then to the life of transformative energy.

I recently attended heavy metal rock concerts two nights in a row. First was Iron Maiden (arising from Birmingham in 1972). They flew in on their own jumbo jet and put on a great, high-quality, strong, well-managed performance. Bruce Dickinson, the lead vocalist, talked at the end, that it was all about the people and the music, and gave reference to the sorry state of worldwide warring conflicts. The emphasis was on the loss of spiritual power to control war games.

The following night Ozzy Osbourne of Black Sabbath fame produced a master display of music that originated from East London in 1968. One might have expected TV malaise, but this was a masterful Ozzy performance, solid to the core of Black Sabbath music. It was carried on good skill and intonation of the spiritual soul.

The crowd was excited and respectful of both groups. There was spirit in the air.

These are good times of the stirring of the inner being. It has to come from self, because that is the only explanation for a staid audience member standing with effervescence when stirred at key points of the performance. The soul is being moved.

I liked that Prashant, a young Nepalese student I met at the Iron

Maiden concert, was ecstatic and moved with energy, making this his greatest day! He had only recently traveled from Nepal, having experienced the disastrous earthquakes of that country a year back. With the modern age cell phone camera, he recorded scenes of the concert, which would make someone's day back in Nepal.

From music, the heavens can open up, and the journey is one for the soul. Bear in mind the great concerts you have attended and feel the power of the music that has carried forward with you. Great music is always from the soul. It is intuitive. The music floats in.

CHAPTER 32

HOW CAN YOU BE HAPPY?

It comes from within. As much as the outer world is relevant, immense gratitude to life comes from within. It's tied to the mojo, the magical charm of life, inner heightened enlightenment, a bountiful amount of intuition.

Be peaceful and want just for now to be focused on nice stuff. I'm about to go to bed. I'm rereading the book on the life of surfer Clay Marzo and am looking forward to the next section. Satisfaction before sleep. I'm mindful of the day offering up such pleasant things. Happiness can be found in an interesting, good book.

It is also a way to quiet the mind and focus on fewer things. Less clatter. If you have good intentions and think and carry out goodwill, you will receive good karma in return, as there is a fine web of interconnectedness. Doing for others is a way to get great thrills and satisfaction.

You cannot just hang in with thoughts of past happenings. Find the moment that is going to please you the most. When you chat in the early morning about what you will wear that day, who are you talking with? Your self-energy, the real you, your external ego's "roommate" voice.

The other voice you have in you, needs to be quieted so that the real you can get along fine with yourself. Calm things down. A short mindfulness exercise will help calm you, if, say, a coworker, a fellow commuter, a loved one, or some other person has transgressed on your happiness zone … what to do?

Love yourself. Quiet things. Get your personal space in order. Make a list of notes telling yourself what you want to do that can lead to happiness. In other words, what will get the best results? If you are only self-focused, you will not get as much happiness as if you focus to help others. This will bring you greater happiness.

Eat some good food and do some favorite exercise. Enjoy yourself.

This is all understood by motivators and therapists to encourage you to explore the biggest and best of all that is good in you. To freshen up to this you need to get inside your being, know your intuitive self, overcome limitations of yourself, and discover afresh where you are going.

In the psychology world this might be called self-actualization, but move to the spiritual world and you want to explore your intuitive side, your heart, soul, subconscious attributes. This is a new journey, and there are lots of ways you can get there and be happy. Start with what's on this page.

Mind and heart in harmony are like a beach in sultry conditions—the hum of the surf and warmth of the setting sun. Happy-happy.

Picnic, share food, take a walk. The world is your palette. Seek nature. Share a smile with others. The happiness in the world will come from within you, as much as other people may help you along the way.

CHAPTER 33

ENERGY READING INTUITION

Finding place was more than just having places but coming to feel that the oneness of energy means we all share that which is universal, infinite consciousness, the universe in us.

It's there. I can't see it, but I can feel it. Touch, a strength of mine, feeling in my hands, knowing that I can use that to communicate with what has become obvious. Yes, obvious. Wow! Others do not think this way? Well, we shall explore.

I just went to a finish-up function for a local yoga center, one that had the focus on a daughter who was specialized in that level of yoga and which was placed in a purpose reconstructed center for the generating of good bodywork and good harmony with the elements that we know of as yoga. That means we can enhance our soulfulness and feel good about our day. Maybe it is as close to soothing our soul, next to being with nature. Soothe your soul this way, and everything else will become easier. That's why we exercise. It is to develop within, so we can develop outside as well.

What have you got to lose if you seek answers from within? Do you need to feel that inner self before you try to commune with it? If it doesn't fit a slot in your thinking, make a gesture of openness and you will receive in return. If you're not open, you won't receive.

Explore it? Call it Zen. It is the passage you travel that adds a depth of relating to yourself and to any writing or creative exercise you do. Have faith in being Zen. You won't know it, but you will move distances in your being, and you will ride the waves to your own deeper fulfillment.

Surfers know this place. Silence in a tube, the sudden rush of sound as you move to the open wave; stresses and never-ending head conversations go away. You are meditative because of nature.

Ask for it.

Be open to it.

Get to feel hot hands. Then you will know the spirit world is visiting you!

At the yoga function, it was a wholesome time. People shared good talk and common energies.

Chris was a communications technology scientist who enquired about my business. I initially didn't ask him about his. We talked of my writing and the genre. That's, Meta. Hmmm. We chatted around the realm of life where we have faith to ask and listen, breathe, and feel the inner self as it communicates as your intuition. It will empower you and make you wiser. Many know this field, and many can open themselves to have it find them.

The great thing is that when you hang out, commune, chatter, discuss philosophies, create new things with like people, make great music, and establish a great garden as your canvass, you will interact without need to question or to make unnecessary critiques or challenges to the person or being with whom you converse. Spiritually aware open people will find ease with similar others. It's pretty cool!

I like to focus on simpler interpretations of the spiritual world, like being in the garden when baby birds are finding their wings with their mothers' encouragement. It is not a complex thing to get to better know your intuition. I write about the passage of our lives. There are echelons of ways and time that provide for your individual passage, but we all share the same energy, the universe within ourselves that will be the guidance we need. If you don't open to it, you don't get it.

The greatness of discussion with a like-minded person is comforting. There is no attrition. You reach the heights of greater self-awareness, like at the level of self-actualization on Maslow's Hierarchy of Needs.

Abraham Maslow created a hierarchy of needs over five tiers. He was looking at motivation. You are where life is more meaningful. The passage takes you up the hierarchy:

- self-actualization;
- esteem;
- love and belonging;
- safety; an
- physiological

Authors like Dr. Dyer advise us to seek Source. This is the passage you are on. Seek it. Dyer considered that we all have access to this level at the top of Maslow's Hierarchy. It is approachable. It leads you to your full potential.

How do you get there? Set some goals outside of your own self, have faith in accessing its energy, have feelings for those you can relate to, share the energy, and explore your spirituality. You know, like a little birdie told you—and the aha moments of your life.

Finding passage is the key to adventure, making the most out of life, your life, the spiritual dimension, your real life!

CHAPTER 34

UBER COOL

All good things can happen.

I was driving down Fendalton Road in Christchurch on a summer day in my little Morris Minor van when a euphoric state came over me that lifted me to the echelons of greatness of my inner being. Just a way of saying I felt great! The reason was that a long run of university exams had come to an end, and the pent-up stress was released. Oh, my Lord. The universe provided a sweet spot. We were in days when a year's university study was assessed in two or three exam papers over three hours per subject. No continuous assessment in unit form, as the format would go to. Three exams over two days, of nine hours' exam time total, was a fair chunk of a year's work assessment. It was of no surprise that my body would apprise itself of relief and euphoria on Fendalton Road that day. Interestingly, it remains a strong memory so many decades on. You do get great states of being, and they have to come from the inner energy of our subconscious, our soul, our intuitive realm.

This is a culmination of inner sanctity. It is divineness, times that are holistic and exhilarating due to hard work, focus, and pulling together all the outer and inner skills you can rely on. There is exhilaration, empowerment, and self-awareness.

If you're younger, you might be better tempted to follow the style world. Style core attributes, like design quality, come from within.

We all notice things that have a zing. The realm of nature works in a harmonious legend. It is bespoken to naturalness that we admire, absorb the greatness of natural landscape, play fully in the midst of things that are attractive because they are. They are the combination of how the universe formed things for us. We are attracted because we welcome having that in our lives. Walk in any garden, realizing that a garden is never finished, so the bounty is always more to come! We welcome and admire being able to swathe ourselves in nature.

Discussing style as a notion with young media students, I found a sense that we know what that style is. Something is stylish. Someone wears something that is stylish. An artifact has a certain style, even of agelessness. What is the realm of style that we learn to create? How do forms come together and excite us in their newness, uniqueness, colorfulness, harmony, and all manner of things that just signal style?

A person labeled as jazzy from the style of dress and manner of life will suggest he or she acts and dresses in a lively way.

We should always honor the individual who says something and stands for something. Tell those who do things of significance, who test boundaries, genuinely how they are respected.

It is wonderful when things come together in a way that all things fit. Life can be the sum of all good things! Great moments occur in a life!

I was at Sydney Airport en route back from Asia, where color and style is always to the fore. The eastern touch. Try it, you'll like it! I was spending time at the airport en route to New Zealand, and after one of those wearying stretch-out-the-best-you-can plane discomforts, there was that enlightening moment that draws your attention. A young Aussie surfer boy had arrived off a flight and met up with a friend to connect to another flight. To all the weary and scruffy air travelers around the terminal, here was this stylish young boy, and the cosmos opened up.

In light-green trousers, blond hair, white T-shirt, black shoes, and brown socks, he looked cool. Carried an iPad, had a suntan. Seized on some fashion senses. Thank you, Aussie surfer boy. You brought together some elements of a life that raised spirit to a combination of things that just say, self, I have something together. For he had decided those elements and made a day great for his day traveling.

CHAPTER 35

PEOPLE I HAVE KNOWN

It is wise to take stock of people around you. You may overlook the intuitive counsel that they can provide. Look closely at people you know to explore your intuition.

Paul was a defense lawyer in a famous mass murder trial. I knew this guy at university. We worked in a freezing meat plant in our summer holidays. His father, the boss of the company, visited sometimes. We hid behind the meat carcasses. I didn't think much of it then, the life of animals taken for the food chain. We needed money to enable study to continue on at university.

I recently drove past that area and took a wrong turn. Found us back in the stockyards. A young black bobby calf raised its lonesome head and looked intently for all the time at us. I froze in my inner soul. It was life to be taken. I had failed. Should have jumped into the pen and taken it home as a pet in my Volvo, Cabriolet hood down!

Who knows whether David Bain was guilty of mass murder? This was a case where the father, mother, son, and daughter were all killed in Dunedin, New Zealand. Was it the father, or the son, David Bain. You couldn't understand how someone could do that to his whole family. David had allegedly been out delivering morning newspapers, but only he knows the truth. The trial made it what it was. I just expect it of him. He was unwell after having presented the case to the Privy Council in London. These things have huge demands and huge repercussions. Good people have to stand up! The police did not do the best analytical investigation. The jury found him not guilty. My attorney friend Paul was a key member on the defense team. Knowing his work ethic, I expected he would have done the source work leading to the trial's success. I am happy to say that on a recent catch-up, he is still a sweet man with an acute mind, the same considerate man that he was as a young guy at university.

Look at your friends. Do they have things to teach you? Will they stand the test of time? Will there be a day when you can respectfully say he or she is my good friend?

Della Newman, accompanied by her husband, Wells McCurdy, was the US ambassador to New Zealand under US president George Bush Sr. We need to get that right! I know two people, close friends, who worked for US presidents. It seemed true that the inside comments of White House staff were that Ronald Reagan and George Bush Sr. were great men to work for. They were personable, humorous, and dignified around the executive building and oval office, regardless of external world politics.

I joined up with a Seattle friend, and we crashed a congratulations ceremony that was held on the announcement of Newman's appointment. It was held in the Boeing Air Museum just south of downtown Seattle. We joined the line to meet her and offer congratulations, and when I reached Della, I told her I was from the sister city in New Zealand. The staffer was ushering me on, but she insisted we talk. Friendships were made and kept over her time. We laughed together.

Della was private friends with President Bush Sr. and his family, and they holidayed together. On the day that the United States went to war in Iraq over the invasion of Kuwait, the president had no appointments, except one: Della. That's what friends do, and what was said is private, but you can imagine that warm regard for international friendship with New Zealand and its people was part of it. You never just know where your energies, life force, connections, and sharing go. Go live life! Be open to it!

We sat in a little group of eight in the University of Washington in Seattle listening to a woman backbench parliamentarian who was traveling on fact finding and experience gathering in between sessions of parliament in New Zealand. Now she, Helen Clark, is a world leader. I'm pleased that she has had time as third in charge in the United Nations as the head of economic development, that she has been able to live away from New Zealand since being that country's prime minister and was able to savor the life of a New Yorker. This is the living culture where you can open your mind, explore others' beliefs, develop rational investigations, and be yourself.

Lester Woods was a prudent man. A West Coaster. he made cautious but good investments. As university students, we rented a house from him. We struck up a conversation that was more than a conversation. He gave me an antique copper concave heater that I still have. Lester took to training and racing horses. He looked upon me as a bright-minded university boy, even though my best scholarliness, I feel, came later in my life.

He came by to ask what he should feed his horses. I was a cross-country runner at the university, and we had talked about carbohydrate diets during training, the idea being that we would eat little bread, potatoes, and such things for some days and then overload for several days before an event. I was always scrambling to get training time in.

One night while training, I disturbed a thief breaking into a nurse's car outside the hospital. As I ran by, I asked the thief, "Is this your car?"

"Yeah, yeah," he muttered.

"It can't be," I said. "It belongs to a friend of mine!"

We took off running, me after him. A taxi driver called the police. I was teaching at the time, and when I told some junior students in a high school, they seemed rather incredulous. I wasn't sure what morality they were demonstrating.

What did I know about horse food? I told Lester he needed to get the carbs, proteins, and fats right.

"Like what?" he asked.

From then on horses got a daily cooked mash of potatoes, corn maize, and other good additions. They were well cared for.

Lester called to tell my family that his latest horse was running in the big race on Saturday and that he had named it after me. "What?" I asked. His name was Able Tim, they said! Well, that could be deserving, but I had to be humble; as much as Lester Woods had put faith in me, I was intrigued.

Off to the race course we went, and there in the final bend was Able Tim—and it was to be Able Tim first past the post!

I walked back with the horse. We were new mates. He seemed to kind of know me. Well, that's what I thought. There's more to this than good tucker food, there was a huge dollop of sensitive care and attention by a good man. I think his sister June had a big part to play in that too.

We all live in a multi-connected world. We are all one. Keep your eyes open.

Bernie is an engineer, a rugged type who speaks in a voluble and staccato way. He's the professor really and wickedly aware of the inner spiritual dimension. This is akin to those people on Earth who don't get recognized because people around them can't see the truly great qualities that are within. So much ordinariness in this world. Bernie likes the spiritual self-help story of *Jonathan Livingston Seagull*, a novella by Richard Bach about a mythical seagull trying to soar to new heights.

We took a road trip, one of those events that you need to give energy to, plan and activate some things, and give it your all. Bernie is a great road tripper. Full of enthusiasm and offering. Loves talks and chats. He followed up on things in the days following. He learns, shares, and takes and gives wisdom in a Bernie sort of way.

You might imagine there are Bernie's in this world you need to open up and listen to. Be open to them!

Bernie likes the spiritual and self-help story of *Jonathan Livingston Seagull*. This was a novella of a mythical seagull trying to soar to new heights. Bernie calls me Fletcher. He just knows. Don't underrate people out of hand!

It's great that people can come into your life, even if they leave, but there will be a fair chance that they will return. Life cycles like that. Tanz, Paula's partner, is that kind of fellow. Knew him in Seattle, met him again in China and then in New Zealand and then back in Seattle. He is a New Zealand native Maori and greets you with a *hongi*, the touching of noses, that goes deeper than any handshake. Quality guy.

Paula is a unique being in this world. She knows before she is aware and finishes her e-mails with "we are all one."

You love being around Paula because she brings lightness and being. She has a wonderful talent for making cards to acknowledge when something pretty cool is happening. I got pretty tired of organizing my own birthdays, so a handful of years back I left it to someone else. Does it work? Sometimes. This last time around some great friends, Jan, Di, Paula, and Matt and Lisa from Seattle joined in a function arranged by my editor assistant Jan Hadfield, at the Untouched World Café & Native Garden Restaurant in Christchurch. They display the unique garments that Bill Clinton and other international citizens loved to wear. Great occasion. Best start to a day I could remember. Super, super—and then there was the card!

Paula makes a montage of words and pictures that sum up a person's inner being. She has that wonderful touch. I got a super card to cherish and acknowledge, that this person had well understood me, that on my day of birth I was recognized for what I have and what I have become, and what I feel is important in a wise life.

Time and thought has been given.

In my card from Paula on my birthday, she included: You are divine love.

"See the light in others, and treat them as if that is all you see"—Dr. Wayne Dyer.

"To the world you may be one person, but to one person you may be the world"—John Lennon.

"We all want to be famous people and the moment we want to be someone, we are no longer free"—Jiddu Krishnamurti.

"In oneself lies the whole world and if you know how to look and learn, the door is there and the key is in your hand. Nobody on earth can give you either the key or the door to open, except yourself"—Jiddu Krishnamurti.

Judy Brown was a truly inspired guide to finding good things. She does it so well that you almost forget to say thank you. Judy is an author and a teacher, and with her late husband, Jack, who was a psychiatrist, managed a number of good service projects, helping others around the world.

She made the arrangement possible for me to be a teacher on the faculty at Lakeside School in Seattle, Washington. New life was everywhere. It was a great experience.

Thank you to the above people for being you.

Have you looked around and noticed the qualities of the people in your life?

CHAPTER 36

GREAT ORATORS OF INTUITION

(Quotes in this chapter are from Dr. Wayne Dyer's Maui presentation in 2015 and his Auckland presentation in 2015).

Finding passage in life comes in ways and dimensions through life experience. There are significant points and people to signal the journey. In the case of Dr. Wayne Dyer, it was interesting because my passage of being more alert to intuition in our lives and my writings, prior to learning of his genre and style, are very much the same journey. It was suddenly part of my journey when I first heard him talk, and I was there when he gave his last presentation, as he died two days later.

Dr. Dyer, who has written for Hay House publishers, was an author who gave guidance to spiritual growth and self-help for personal development. Listening to him talking to his many enthusiastic followers was filled with knowledge and understanding that gave focus to how you could overcome weaknesses in our personal lives. He gave us ways forward to improve our sense of empowerment.

When I was at university I knew of his book *Your Erroneous Zones*. I didn't get to read it until another forty years had passed. I had an academic and teaching career for much of that time.

I was surfing in Maui in November 2014 and spent a little

catch-up time in Seattle before heading to New York and staying from Christmas through New Year. I called a bookshop in Seattle that had been referred to me as a place to find spiritual books. It was great. Good energy and a good feel pervaded that place. The head buyer advised me of several book publishers who best served them. I tried to connect with them, but not to great success. I must have touched in with Hay House, who published Wayne Dyer. They were to beckon.

I discovered a book event in Maui, and as I sometimes live in Kahana and surf in that area, I saw sense in flying from New Zealand, where I was based, to attend. Like all intuitive decision making, the mind wanders around the topic until the intuitive read directs you to a decision.

It's a gift, the leap of consciousness that puts you in a place that didn't need a rational think to get there. It's genius! You can build on an intuitive bug, and with practice a whole new world opens up.

That was about to happen for me with Wayne Dyer. I later realized that he'd spent time nearby in Maui. For me the final decision to attend the event was assured when a Hay House counsel agent assured me that it was right up my alley.

Arriving by car in Maui, I entered my ocean lookout apartment at Kahana. I took a shower and then put on gray slacks, a clean white shirt, a silver Thai-styled jacket, and leather shoes. I found the car park, walked a fair bit, arrived several minutes' after it had started, and there was Wayne Dyer, commanding attention.

Jeff came over to me at the end of that day. "Can I introduce myself?" he said. "You stand out."

Hmm, the silver-gray jacket?

"You looked somewhat anguished, frown on your face."

I was deeply intrigued at the format and response of Wayne Dyer and Hay House fans, who were in hog heaven. Who, what, when, where, why, and how, from being a journalism teacher, were covered, among other things.

Jeff and his partner were to connect over lunch by the seaside. Turtles were at play alongside in the foaming surf. I'm sure we'll meet again in New Zealand and, I expect, elsewhere. People who have reached oneness, a bigger spiritual sense and honed intuitive skills at work, have a collective gift. You won't argue, as the realm is too heavenly. It was an interesting three days.

Dyer took center stage for much of it. He was certainly profound. Ensconced in a leather chair, sporting a beret, he gave a skilled delivery. Calm assurance that the energy of the universe, his Godlike spirit was truly at work. I purchased his biography. There was no opportunity to get it signed. He was always surrounded by energetic supporters. I guess he got used to that.

I read the biography over the next month, annotating using a purple pen, Wayne's favorite writing color, my favorite color, and for me always a purple pen on my desk. I was on the way to discovering a mentor who was 95 percent the genre of my first book in this meta field. I was surprised, to say the least, as I had not read a single item of his. You might be surprised, but in finding passage in a life, some things are just kept in the wings until the student is ready for the teacher to arrive. A Buddhist saying that Wayne Dyer often used. That was true for me, and now I had this biographical feast of a mentor's writings.

I was looking for a new genre for my next book and I became aware that he was to visit Brisbane, Sydney, Melbourne and Auckland. Traveling to Melbourne Ted Talks I was just to miss him, but there was an opportunity in Auckland, New Zealand, where he was to present at an evening in the Aotea center. I had to be there.

I made it. On stage strolls Dr. Wayne Dyer. New Zealanders are somewhat more reserved and laid back to that of US folk. He would have a task and an opportunity to show the pinnacle of his skill and the core of his life belief.

It is divine spirit which is central to his talk. You can say that he puts the inner realm of our life as being able to be reached by people of all levels. He enhances his talk showing audio visual of Andromeda 2.5 million light years away and of an estimated 100 billion galaxies. I feel he makes it comfortable to get conscious of the divine. It is infinite universe and so be our spirit.

I look around the auditorium of the Aotea Center. You can see from people that this speaks to them. Leaning forward, edging onto the front of your seat. Wayne Dyer is at work. a master of spiritual oneness. One daughter sings to us. One daughter tells of a mind/ body/ health experience.

Wayne talks of the children. His book *Memories of Heaven,* with Dee Garnes, is new. He says, "Children teach us that God is in us."

What we know is that the world we actively participate in or observe can be of the ego mind or from our inner being, often referred to as infinite consciousness. When you have self-inquiry or seek insight, you're looking for a place that is beyond the scientific. Being philosophical is okay. Finding a feeling that has greater grandeur in your life, being meditative, is enlightenment and yes, you become a better understanding person. You can liberate yourself by being open to these life energies, and when you take time to listen and study the great world philosophers, you truly can soar. You are at one with life. Universal energy.

His followers nod in acknowledgement. Dr. Wayne Dyer, teacher, spiritualist, and much more, was at work. It is from these masters that you can assist the way you define your own path. Some of the grandmasters, the Indian and Chinese scripts of understanding, for example, can be heady and require academic discourse toward understanding. Someone like Dr. Wayne Dyer can give commonality, understanding, and good sense to what it means to be more understanding of our intuitive sense.

I profile Dr. Wayne Dyer, as he entered my life at a crucial time in my passage to understanding the power of intuition. I was writing in the same genre before I came to know his writing. I felt it was significant.

Wayne started speaking at 6:30 p.m. He wrapped up his presentation at 9:20 p.m. He was due to fly to Hawaii at ten past midnight.

The crowd respectfully left the auditorium. I was guided by that movement outward, and when the theater was empty, I found my way back in and to the stage. Wayne was collecting his books and things and several people had gathered, including his two daughters. A young woman who he had encountered on a walk through a cemetery alongside his hotel, and who had been surprised to realize he was in Auckland, said she had been invited to attend the presentation and had come by to say thank you. She said she had learned so much.

I had a brief time to chat, to tell him I hadn't gotten his signature in his biography when in Maui, that we had mutual friends through a surfer son's fame, and providing a solid purple pen, I received a final signature of Wayne Dyer inside his biography!

He flew to Waikiki, Hawaii, took an onward flight to Maui and then a car journey to his place on the NW coast. He passed in his sleep the next night.

Be your own orator. Find a way to guide your life to inner thoughts, and live from the inner soul and not just from the outer mind. This will happen through human need anyway, so why not add another dimension? Once you open to a greater voice that can guide you, you will accept the guides from within. If you're afraid or resistant to that, you will not share in the energies and understanding that can be your greater guide.

Open to it, learn from it, be with it. Can you, will you, shall you? Once you are comfortable that guides can help you along life's journey, you will better learn how to listen to your intuitive voice.

I was with a friend who was running for a particularly high political office. She asked me if she should run for this office. I said yes, it was there for her and she should just do it. The position was meant to be hers.

She asked, "Do you think so?"

I said, "I know so! Just do it."

All politicians should be better at listening to their spiritual journeys. My friend has been the head elected person. She spoke to me at a much later date and said she found what I said and how I said it a bit freaky. My reply was, "Oh, just think of it as like the natural energy you feel in a really nice garden, and then it will be better understood."

What tells you how to act? The inner path of your sentient life. What leads me to that? Openness, faith, trust—use what you've been given. Follow being open to your inner seer and ask how your inner being can soar. Be like the seagull who soared to greater heights, even though it meant going along his separate path. You can do it. That is why speakers in school assemblies and such give messages that you can do anything you want. A lot of great achievement will come from the power of inner intuitive understanding.

That is also why a lot of great achievers in our lives had less than exemplary passages in getting through school. Bill Gates of Microsoft shown some exemplary behavior as he became aware of the computer language that could be used in machines across the globe. The message can be success and good sustenance. Was intuitive passage a strong point for the success of the Microsoft story? It certainly was in the success of Steve Jobs and Apple and in the understandings of Albert Einstein, who discussed intuition as the most important thing. These are all iconic leaders. Another book is needed to cover this expansive topic.

So how much can people be energized to add to their pathways of life if they discover and open to their greater intuitive energies? Empowerment from this can and should be the pathway for the best human endeavors, yet for many it is never encouraged. That will always happen, of course. Be special and open to your greater journey.

If you want guidance as to how you can better live your life, listen to great leaders What are they saying? Develop new intentions and ways of thinking in your life. Be open to that! The best and greatest political leaders change their minds. Why shouldn't you? Innovative behavior can take people on twists and turns that can drive people crazy with the leader's immense vision. Remember how a pulp mill business became a famous cell phone company! Intuitive energy always provides radiance, so that goes a step further. Together it lights up universal energy. Space exploration in the early twenty-first century will be led by many people in this demanding category. There can be huge plusses and huge challenges when working alongside such brilliance. Get some balance, and be open to the inner intuitive life, and balance and harmony will be empowered.

The intuitive leader won't be happy to do what everyone else does and will seek to stride forth! Contributions by Nelson Mandela, Mahatma Gandhi, Winston Churchill, Martin Luther King Jr., and others are famous for guiding world history. I believe that these people had clear use of intuitive awareness. Just sitting and thinking will provide answers. Take time to find a still, quiet voice.

Among the great successes are people who can handle the great speed of change. Richard Branson, of the Virgin Group, believes if you are going to do it, do it now.

The information deluge has magnified with history, yet these successful leaders manage to control it. What makes the difference? Intuition has to be a big part of such knowledge. Knowing before you know! They will cultivate the 360-degree understanding that I have written about. There are skilled ways to work around obstacles others saw as impossible to transcend. The collective will always be needed. Bosses, be aware that your teams are part of you, and without them, you are nothing.

I'm for empowerment, and the best way to gain this is to be intuitively aware that you can gain, sustain, and enhance what you do by looking for a more enlightened way to serve the people you rely on. If you are only looking at improving the bottom line and overriding opposition, your efforts won't be as great.

I have just visited various places in Great Britain and Europe. Brexit has happened. It doesn't matter what part of these regions and what hemisphere you're in, you will find variance in how people do and don't work to perform better.

For example, shop assistants bug me by not listening and then repeating their "what do you want?" query. They may not take the time to explore how they can help the client and how the strength and power of the customer might add to their lives.

I came in from surfing in Maui one day and called a surf shop in one of the malls. A young woman greeted me and then helped find appropriate clothes that I would like, taking things from the changing room and bringing more clothes to help me choose. Of course, I bought more goods than I would have otherwise. She completed the transaction and then asked if I would write a review. I was happy to write that I had been the owner of a hotel and that this young lady was exemplary.

She walked out with me and asked if she could get something from her car in the staff parking lot. I waited for her to return, and she invited me to later attend a new business development for something I was suited to.

There was a powerful message of what could be achieved here by getting to know your customer. Some people really help make it a great day, don't they? People who just know! This young woman certainly did. More intuitive. A gift for her.

I was at the Edinburgh Arts and Fringe Festival in August 2016. I was caught trying to find the venue of a friend's performance. Many cobblestone streets and many enquiries to locals got me to the university square where the event was, but it was over. I counted the number of enquiries I made: twenty-nine. Of those, I was guided to seven different venues. Some were keen to help but didn't know. Quite a number were defensive, as they didn't know. A small number went quite outside what you would expect and helped, and this as always along with a sense that they wanted to help and this drove their sense of support. They were young, wore the purple tops that signified official participation, and were the true bounty that that city provided on the day.

To the dark-haired boy all by himself in the formal information booth in George Square, and the young woman outside the rear entrance to the performance of *Jane Eyre*—you both are magic! I'm pretty confirmed in my thinking that they were just intuitively smart!

When there is confusion because information or time to carry out usual processes is lacking, the greater intuitive use to make progress can be without seeking others' guidance, as there is already a wide source of intuitive understanding. Being wise will guide you to people around you who make use of intuitive energy. You don't want people to second guess.

Everyone can use their intuition to greater levels than they do. It's just nature. When you look to the leaders, you will see natural life energy at work, and this energy is available to all of us. It is your decision whether you will be more open to it. We all have it! Expanded thinking will not be linear. Grow your vision. To gain the higher ideals of self, lead to greater achievement of the greater good that you can do for yourself and for others. We will never achieve all that we can, but we will achieve more highly if we choose to use intuitive understanding. Timeless ideas of human potential are there for us.

Leadership is very much a trait of intuitive understanding. Being open to intuition and learning about it and how you can participate will enhance leadership potential. This field of what makes a great leader might be wide open to understanding the many forces that hone the behavior of people in lead positions. The real challenge will be to have these people be open to trusting the intuitive forces within all of us. We must trust in our feelings. This will be even more necessary when things change rapidly around us. Observe people's behavior when this happens, and you will see those who intuitively grasp the way forward against those who flap about the many small points that they are trying to mold into some structure to move forward. Sometimes there is no way forward, just levels of understanding of the situation and how any of these can help with a better handling of where you are.

Experience and age are precursors to openness to greater trust in intuitive life and hence a better resolution. It is not information only that will provide for better answers but the combining of cognitive skill with intuition. This will make you much more powerful in managing life.

CHAPTER 37

TEA ON A TEAL MORNING

Easy, confident, and swaggering could be descriptions of the Kiwi culture of New Zealand that I grew up with. I always liked repatriating onto a teal-blue Air New Zealand flight, seeing Kiwi people returning home. What you want in a population is a good education level, great skills, motivated entrepreneurship, and the logic to handle financial activity. New Zealand is a farming country, and the rural culture probably explains that swagger and easygoing manner. As we go through life, the passage provides many challenges. Ill health matters, and when a person experiences numerous illnesses, there is an accumulation of effects to the body. Life can be more of a challenge.

The University of Otago's Dunedin Multidisciplinary Health and Development Study of a large group of one thousand newborn babies throughout their lives from 1972 has provided a worldwide multitude of research papers and top health stories from highly regarded universities. It tells us so much about the reality of living, the being of life.

What we have learned is that a good start in life is everything about future health. It provides for lower incidences of conditions such as schizophrenia and heart disease. The opposite is a life where youngsters are stressed by poorer upbringing.

The study reports that at thirty-eight years of age, the cardiovascular age ranged from twenty-five to sixty-five years old. As we age, we have varying decreasing capabilities and incidences of ill health. This study has overridden the earlier nature versus nurture discussion. It seemed appropriate that if someone had music skills and had access to a piano, a teacher could guide that person to musical success. I see the study as confirming that it's not so much nature—our genetics—but nurture, the conditions in which the baby is brought up.

But above that, it is the tipping into action the health processes that bring ill health into a life? What are these tipping mechanisms? Why do they activate when they do? These questions are now being further researched.

In the intuitive life, that which pertains to the non-physical and supernatural of our lives, there is a constant flow of positive energy. It's always sunny there. It doesn't change for rich or poor. It is universal and all being. A person who opens to a sense of oneness of life of all living things will be empowered to a strengthened lifestyle. As the physical energy of descending health through life makes itself know, the intuitive spirituality, metaphysical life, and inner peace increase in our enlightenment to it. That is why soulfulness and wisdom are worth further exploration. It can be an ageless time. Some young people are exceptionally wise.

You will find great masters and directional guides throughout history, including Leonardo da Vinci; Charles Darwin; Albert Einstein; Mahatma Gandhi; Bill Gates; Steve Jobs; Martin Luther King Jr.; John Lennon; Nelson Mandela; Michelangelo; the migrant mother in *The Grapes of Wrath*; Sir Isaac Newton; Plato; Aristotle; Elvis Presley; Mother Teresa; Catherine the Great; Queen Victoria; Marie Curie; Rosa Parks; Burmese politician, diplomat, and author Aung San Suu Kyi; Oprah Winfrey; Dalai Lama; Richard Branson; Oscar Wilde; Sigmund Freud; and Anne Frank. Many are noted through Western media. There are Indian, Chinese, and other cultures well represented in the greatness of their iconic people.

A great teacher of what life is all about is Jiddu Krishnamurti, and his well-known writing in *Freedom from the Known.* He says people seek "something beyond ourselves." He adds, "Has life any meaning at all? The learning in life is."

CHAPTER 38

UNLEASHING YOUR INTUITION

Just start. Eyes and ears open. Use your senses. Train your subconscious. Relax your logical mind. Surf your thoughts. The intuitive energy and information will always be there. It is unlimited. Write a problem down. Wait as needed—solutions will come. How or why is unsure, but it will come.

Einstein says, "The intuitive mind is a sacred gift and the rational mind a faithful servant. We have created a society that honors the servant and has forgotten the gift."

There is an intuitive bug you can get that helps you understand your inside; listen to your inner voice. Life is a constant inner voice discussion, as if you were talking to a roommate.

Consider all the aspects of the day. What shall I wear, who might I meet, what is likely to take place, how would I best handle such an occasion? and so on.

To get to the inner voice, you should do away with the clatter of head talk, the cognitive thinking. Focus on your thoughts and feelings. Write them down in a diary or journal, as this will help capture your thoughts.

Listen to what is going on in your life without judgment. Ignore the inner critic. Some people describe this as being wise to your inner voice. Work on quietness and a calm disposition. You are seeking a clear, sentient pathway. A mentor or "energy reader" will provide practical help. Look for and ask a person of such stature who can help you.

Creativity can be a great help. Maybe you dance, enjoy music, a quiet place to read, writing poetry, exercising, playing an instrument, or singing. Bring some color and style into your life.

Design something. Recreate your living space. That is why qi (chi) energy is important in how we live. Real estate people will say a great house is reflective of the energy of the people who live there, and their decisions and attitudes to how they organize their living space will create energy that stays, even when they have moved on.

Chi is the energy of heaven and earth, or in New Zealand native Maori culture, heaven is Rangi and Earth is Papa. According to Maori mythology, heaven and earth were once joined. Ringinui, the Sky father, and Papatuanuku, the Earth mother, held each other in an embrace but were forced apart, and humanity came to exist. Life was found. It is all-encompassing, and if you are open to it, you will furnish to a much higher level of style coordinates, as well as spiritual awakening.

I live in a house that is older than one hundred, so there has been some time for many people to leave their mark. The house has been altered and developed over the years. Guests say they like the space, and we have some nice times.

But it has changed. I arrived back from India at the turn of the century to find a man peering into the side window. He was apologetic. He explained that he once spent time in this house when it was a Buddhist retreat. He now runs such a place in England, but that day he lightened my energy by explaining that part of the house's history. It didn't surprise me.

There are aha moments in our lives when intuitive energy is strong. There is instant awareness as information comes from intuition to our consciousness. This eureka moment is all the brainpower, including the right side of the brain, the visualizing impact, that is from inner intuitive feeling. You will ride high and be empowered by this.

When you feel this empowerment, you are living at a higher level, a life lived more from your subconscious. The implicit learning is happening without your knowing it. Just sigh, be open, and unleash yourself! Your body knows, as you have the biological roots to intuitive thought.

Just as I found that my body was very clear about what was required when I carried out a heavy physical training load for competing in an Ironman triathlon, your body will lead you. Listen to it! Listen with your senses. I say,

Stop looking
(it is in you)
start listening
open to inspiration
allow the answer to find you.

We have a lot of sayings that are intuitive reading in life:

- Follow your nose—trust the senses, just as animals do so well;
- Know the way the wind blows—when we apply our shrewdness to a situation;
- Feel it in your bones—when the weather affects people;
- A little bird told me—the intuitive sense: Is it a secret? When a bird flies into your house, it is time to read that weather or seasonal changes are coming. Perhaps there is a greater message.

My mother, Joy, was adept at playing the piano by ear. She was able to pick up a tune and turn it into a performance piece. There was no written music. It just felt good.

What happens? Where does gifted, intuitive behavior come from? Listen for the song to appear in your mind. Is that how John Lennon and Paul McCartney's "Yesterday" came to be?

Be open to inspiration.

Let the energy find you!

Unleash yourself from within.

Health affects mind, body, and spirit.

There are avenues here to change your well-being, balance your lifestyle, save your life. People are like an instrument. We are stimulated. Exercise. Go walking through gardens. Rest. Take time out. Find food that enhances enjoyment (nice food—you know, the good stuff). Feed your thoughts. Seek intuitive behavior.

Following being involved in a disastrous earthquake that saw 80 percent of central city buildings demolished, we all felt a loss of identity. What was there before in that now empty lot? Simplicity of lifestyle was a panacea.

Good food and wine, discussion, and sharing the load among friends—and from all that, a silver lining appears of better reliance on self, of understanding to accept and deal with the consequences of disaster, and a new pathway of life ensues.

Finding passage in this time is very much helped by asking for answers to your problems and being alert to hear the answers. At least write a bunch of questions in a journal or on a piece of paper before you go to bed. You probably won't find a random list of lottery numbers, but you will find life.

CHAPTER 39

SOME PATHWAYS WITH
UNIQUE MESSAGES

Where do vision and wisdom of the future come from? Is ancestry the source of wisdom?

Ngaa Rauuira Pumanawawhiti is the teenager central to the New Zealand film *Maori Boy Genius*, directed by Pietra Brettkelly. It looks at coming of age, yet the themes go much deeper. Even ancestry seems only part of the answer. Ngaa Rauuira's name translated means "the energy around where lightning strikes." One should look for energy, which is even more guidance from whence the purple reign of the future that comes upon us is found!

Sixteen-year-old Ngaa Rauuira is a youngster of the old spiritual world who is able to live handsomely among his peers. He has leadership potential and accepts the mantle like the Dalai Lama. He studies at a summer program at Yale University.

From where does one's powers in life arise? There is no seemingly foolproof way to find your passage in life. It is an exploration of opportunities and how you handle them. So often the downtimes can only be understood as the precursors to finding and making the grade to the great times. Not one without the other. The yin and the yang.

John Bratton wrote the song "Teddy Bears' Picnic" in 1907. A US composer, he would not have fathomed the global reach of his talent. Irishman Jimmy Kennedy of Taunton, Somerset, wrote the lyrics in 1932. A wooded area by Staplegrove Church was the inspiration for the song, according to folklore. Neither man would have seen its spread, finding its way worldwide and being used for more than thirty years by BBC audio engineers from 1930, to test and calibrate the frequency response of audio equipment. Are we anything more than good vibrations of universal existence? At least the Beach Boys have us on the right path!

Let the unheard from speak. From our intuition we spiritually live alongside other people, even when we are not physically with them? For example, I felt strongly about an Afghan family of political refugees seeking new passage of life and peace, even though I hadn't met them. The answer is within all of us. Wars and conflicts are of the rational mind. People find reasons for attacking others. Should answers to our living be found within, the sacred gift is unleashed, the answer being within us, and war could be no more. Simple individual acts of friendship become acts of freedom. Youth want to live without wars! Education provides the answer.

The political zeitgeist will need to provide the political shifts for the future and can be an answer. The true answer is within ourselves.

CHAPTER 40

INTUITIVE PATHWAYS TO THE FUTURE

If we follow the concept of universal divine energy as a pathway to the future, then problems that are universal will be provided a solution. We will achieve amnesty from the sectoral thinking we see so much of in the twenty-first century: the closing of communities from the move to globalization, the fervent beliefs that drive groups to terrorism in the name of their own religious forms, and the withdrawal from collective support due to people feeling aggrieved that they are no longer included.

Answers to world problems can lie in empowerment, by being in touch with our intuitive self. There have to be universal strands, which when we join with them, the power to change will be meaningful to all. I seek from the Maori word *Mahana*, the light of the sun, that there is always an energy, without fail, that we can use to drive our life. Mahana means "fiery in temperament, but warm and giving of life." Psychic power, really. It is being joyful for others and bearing burdens for them.

Receptive people who listen and become peacemakers are people who have harmony and a desire to establish balance.

They are intuitive.

They show patience.

People who could be called or are in witness of Mahana see that their needs are complimentary to those of others, and they create the needed relationships. It's a blueprint for life into the future.

The novel *Bulibasha: King of the Gypsies,* by Witi Ihimaera, Fulbright Scholar and noted author, has been made into a film called *Mahana,* which tells of the rivalry of two Maori New Zealand sheep-shearing families living on the East Coast area of New Zealand's North Island. It's a story about poverty, family power balance, and domestic violence, and it has strong ties of Maori to the land and animals. It is a story of finding your way through adversity. It has a look at past times through a soft lens, such that we find ourselves reminiscing of times in the past.

We all wish for happiness. The future realm should be different from what it is, according to the theme of the film. We don't need to have violent clashes, lives lived from strictures built up in poverty, dogma, hierarchies of paternalistic attitudes; it's not a good place for kids without peace and harmony.

We do need to carry on for others with joy and be intuitive to the ways we can better empower ourselves. We need a place for all, when people everywhere have some strong bonds with others, without loneliness. This can affect all ages, as in not having a positive sense of life is to see greater cases of ill health and a shortened life. The Mahana approach is to empower yourself, feel that problems are not insurmountable, and know inner life can be like light from the sun. It can and will sustain you onward.

It's attitudinal, taking inner feelings and carrying them forth in the ego world that relates our identity to the world around us.

I spend time living in a small Hawaiian enclave in Maui called Kahana. It has tourist resort visitors. The local boats, a small supermarket, homes of varying types and trades people going about their workday allow it to hum along as a hamlet on the seashore. I think you could find all elements of a harmonious world in a place like Kahana. There are ways we can coexist. We need effort to focus to these.

"Only love can drive out hate"—Martin Luther King Jr.

"Change opinions, erode old barriers, build new structures"—John F. Kennedy.

"Peace can only come from understanding"—Albert Einstein.

Peace is gradual, it cannot be forced, and hate cannot drive out hate. Violence ends up defeating itself.

"How wonderful it is that nobody need wait a single moment before starting to improve the world!"—Anne Frank.

If you collectively work with a small group of thoughtful and committed people, you will create change. It happened on 911, negatively unfortunately, and so did many others working like this for positive change.

A "love and happiness" search on Google brought up 156,000,000 responses in .68 of a second.

There are 72,100,000 responses in Google to "intuitive ways to the future."

These include

- learning to use your hidden intuition;
- spirituality in your life;
- spiritual direction;
- science of mind;
- what your intuition wants you to know/tips to access it;
- ways to strengthen your intuition;
- psychic abilities and how they work;
- spirit guides; and
- how to listen to your intuition.

You have to know your future to be a futurist.

What this means for you is that you work with a heightened mediumship that you have had from birth or you work to reorganize your inner self and develop new skills to read this energy. You want to establish cognizance that allows you to know something without knowing how you know. You must see the future in aha terms and not be restricted to cause/response understandings only. You will still get plenty of practice at doing that. There is lots of information on how to do that. Research social media.

"May your life unfold with ease"—Buddhist prayer.

About the Book

Einstein said, "The intuitive mind is a sacred gift, and the rational mind a faithful servant. We have created a society that honors the servant and has forgotten the gift."

Into the Pure … is about the passage of life based on intuition. It is about one man's finding the knowing before you know, and how to get empowered.

This is about your hidden power. Learn how to create a better life.

You will understand your inner life compared to your outer ego life. You will come to know how to actuate a better life going forward. It is nature. It is good energy. The sun is always shining within.

About the Author

While living in Christchurch City, New Zealand, Tim Nicholls is still tuned in to the greatness of New York. He has taught in New Zealand and Seattle. You may find him in Hawaii surfing the Honolua Bay waves.

He created the boutique hotel Off the Square in Christchurch, New Zealand. He has a strong creative sense and has conducted business in housing development and construction.

He developed his own school form as a New Zealand International School and later an Edge World Network program. In the UN Year of Conflict Resolution, he developed a program aimed at developing youth voices around the world. As a Fulbright Scholar he studied media and journalism.

He has been a swimmer, an official of national water polo teams, youth development personnel for triathlons in New Zealand, a surfer, Ironman triathlete, and multi-sport participant.

This is his first book.

Printed in the United States
By Bookmasters